BEST EVER BARBECUES

Cookery is moving out of the kitchen and into the garden. Whenever the weatherman predicts sunny skies, barbecues are fuelled, meats marinated and salads tossed in celebration of alfresco entertaining. Whether you are feeding the family with burgers in baps, serving a selection of kebabs for a group of guests or seeking to impress with a whole baked fish, the recipes in this book are certain to fire your imagination.

A JB FAIRFAX PUBLICATION

UK COOKERY EDITOR

Jenni Fleetwood

EDITORIAL

Food Editor: Rachel Blackmore
Assistant Food Editor: Anneka
  Mitchell
Home Economist: Donna Hay
Editorial Coordinator: Margaret Kelly
Sub-editor: Ella Martin

DESIGN

Clive Dorman

PHOTOGRAPHY

Ashley Mackevicius (Australia)
Cover photograph and additional
photographs on pages 6, 11, 19, 20,
21, 23, 25, 53, 56, 57, 59, 65, 67, 74,
75, 77 supplied by
Marshall Cavendish Picture Library,
London

CONTENTS

SNACKS & SUNDOWNERS

While the fire flickers and you wait for the flames to subside, treat your guests to a selection of drinks, dips and delicious nibbles.

◆ ◆ ◆

PARMA MELON WEDGES

1 ripe orange-fleshed melon, such as rockmelon (cantaloupe) or charentais
250 g/8 oz very thinly sliced Parma ham
freshly ground black pepper

1 Cut melon in half and scoop out seeds. Cut each half into eight wedges. Remove skin, then cut each wedge crossways in half.

2 Cut each slice of Parma ham lengthways into three long strips. Wrap one strip around each wedge of melon, if necessary keeping it in place with a toothpick (cocktail stick).

3 Arrange wrapped melon wedges on a serving platter; garnish with a fresh herb sprig. Serve at once or cover closely and refrigerate for up to 2 hours. This starter is traditionally served with a grinding of black pepper, so offer a pepper mill when serving the melon wedges.

Makes 32

GUACAMOLE

1 avocado, halved, stoned and peeled
1 tomato, peeled and finely chopped
2 tablespoons lemon juice
1 tablespoon finely chopped fresh coriander or parsley

1 Place avocado in a bowl and mash with a fork. Alternatively process briefly in a food processor (the dip should retain some texture) and spoon into a bowl.

2 Stir in tomato, lemon juice and coriander or parsley. Serve at once or return avocado stone to bowl and cover surface of guacamole closely. Refrigerate until required, then remove covering and avocado stone, stir guacamole and serve with crudités (see page 6) and tortilla chips for dipping.

Serves 6

Parma Melon Wedges

BITE-SIZED KEBABS

Each recipe is sufficient for 10 skewers. Soak wooden skewers in water for 30 minutes before use.

CUCUMBER AND SCALLOPS
1 clove garlic, crushed
1 spring onion, finely chopped
1 tablespoon finely chopped
   fresh basil
1 tablespoon olive oil
2 tablespoons white wine vinegar
freshly ground black pepper
10 scallops, cleaned, or 1 firm
   white fish fillet, cut into
   2.5 cm/1 in cubes
10 thin slices unpeeled cucumber

CHICKEN AND MUSHROOMS
1 tablespoon lime or lemon juice
1 tablespoon corn oil
pinch chilli powder
1 boneless, skinless chicken
   breast fillet, cut into 10 cubes
5 button mushrooms, halved

1   To make the Cucumber and Scallop Kebabs, place garlic, spring onion, basil, oil and vinegar in a bowl.

2   Add black pepper to taste; whisk well. Add scallops or fish cubes and cucumber slices. Toss to coat, then cover and marinate for 30 minutes.

3   Drain scallops or fish cubes, and cucumber; reserve marinade. Top each cucumber slice with a scallop or fish piece. Thread a wooden skewer through both so that the cucumber folds halfway around the scallop or fish cube.

4   To make the Chicken and Mushroom Kebabs, combine citrus juice, oil and chilli powder in a bowl; mix well. Add chicken and mushroom halves and toss to combine. Cover and marinate for 30 minutes. Drain chicken and mushrooms, reserving marinade. Thread a chicken cube and a mushroom half onto each wooden skewer.

5   Cook the kebabs on a lightly oiled barbecue grill over moderately hot coals, brushing with the appropriate marinade before and during cooking. The scallops will require 2-3 minutes and the chicken 4-5 minutes.

Each recipe serves 10

CRUDITÉS WITH DIPS

2 carrots, cut into batons
½ cucumber, thickly sliced
1 head witloof (chicory), separated
   into leaves
½ red pepper, cored, seeded and
   cut into strips
½ green pepper, cored, seeded and
   cut into strips
12 button mushrooms, trimmed
2 radishes, sliced if large

CREAMY CHEESE DIP
175 g/6 oz cream cheese
4 tablespoons crème fraîche
2 teaspoons lemon juice or to
   taste
4 tablespoons chopped spring
   onions
salt
freshly ground black pepper

TOMATO ANCHOVY DIP
1 x 60 g /2 oz can anchovy fillets,
   drained
2 drained sun-dried tomatoes in oil
1 garlic clove, chopped
3 tablespoons olive oil or oil from
   sun-dried tomatoes
1 teaspoon lemon juice
4 tablespoons mayonnaise
2 tablespoons whipping cream
paprika

1   Prepare the vegetables according to type. Place in separate plastic food bags and crisp in the refrigerator.

2   To make the Creamy Cheese Dip, soften the cream cheese in a bowl, then beat in the remaining ingredients. Garnish with snipped chives, if liked.

3   To make the Tomato Anchovy Dip, place the anchovies, sun-dried tomatoes and garlic in a mortar and grind with a pestle until smooth. Alternatively, use a strong bowl and the end of a rolling pin. Whisk the oil and lemon juice into the mixture, then stir in the mayonnaise and cream. Transfer to a bowl; dust with paprika.

4   Place the bowls on a large platter and arrange the crudités around them.

Serves 6

Crudités with Dips

BARBECUED MUSHROOMS WITH CHILLI BUTTER

20 button mushrooms, stalks removed

CHILLI BUTTER
60 g/2 oz butter, softened
½ red chilli, seeded and finely chopped
½ teaspoon ground cumin
1 tablespoon finely chopped fresh parsley

1 Make the chilli butter by processing all the ingredients in a blender or food processor until smooth. Shape the mixture into a roll, wrap closely and chill until firm.

2 Cut the butter log into 20 pieces and place one piece on each mushroom. Cook on a lightly oiled barbecue grill over hot coals for 4-5 minutes or until butter melts and mushrooms are cooked. Serve at once, with toothpicks (cocktail sticks) for spearing.

Makes 20

Bite-sized Kebabs, Barbecued Mushrooms with Chilli Butter

PINEAPPLE RUM PUNCH

½ cup/125 g/4 oz/caster sugar
½ cup/125 mL/4 fl oz/boiling water
1 cup/250 mL/8 fl oz white rum
¾ cup/185 mL/6 fl oz lemon juice
2 cups/500 mL/16 fl oz/pineapple
   juice
1 cup/250 mL/8 fl oz/orange juice
crushed ice
strawberries and pineapple slices
   to decorate

1   Stir sugar into boiling water until dissolved. When cold place in a large bowl. Add rum and fruit juices. Stir mixture well.

2   Serve on crushed ice in individual glasses, adding a slice of pineapple and a half strawberry to each glass.

Serves 8

VIRGIN ISLAND

**4 slices fresh or drained canned
   pineapple, chopped
2 cups/500 mL/16 fl oz pineapple
   juice
½ cup/125 mL/4 fl oz coconut milk
   (see Cook's Tip, page 14)
4 tablespoons lemon juice**

1   Place pineapple, pineapple juice, coconut milk and lemon juice in a blender or food processor. Process until smooth. Serve over ice in tall goblets.

Serves 4

WHITE STRAWBERRY SANGRIA

**16 strawberries, hulled
4 tablespoons orange juice
4 tablespoons orange liqueur
2 cups/500 mL/16 fl oz white wine
1 tablespoon caster sugar**

1   Place all ingredients in a blender or food processor; process until smooth. Chill, then divide between four large chilled wine glasses. Serve immediately.

Serves 4

MARGARITAS
Illustrated on page 45

4 cups/1 litre/1¾ pt Lime Cooler (right)
½ cup/125 mL/4 fl oz fresh lime juice
pinch salt
1½ cups/375 mL/12 fl oz tequila
½ cup/125 mL/4 fl oz orange liqueur
4-6 ice cubes

1 To make the margarita mixture, place the lime cooler, lime juice, salt, tequila and liqueur in a large jug; stir to combine. Cover and set aside for 30 minutes to allow the flavours to blend.

2 Just before serving, place 2 cups/ 500 mL/16 fl oz of the margarita mixture in a blender. Add ice cubes and blend for 30 seconds.

3 Mix blended mixture with remaining margarita. Serve at once. If you do not have a blender, simply serve the margarita mixture over crushed ice.

Serves 12

Cook's Tip: It is traditional to serve margaritas in salt-rimmed glasses. To salt the rim of a glass, dip it in lime juice, then in salt.

CHAMPAGNE COCKTAILS

4 tablespoons orange liqueur
2 cups/500 mL/16 fl oz champagne

1 Divide the liqueur between four champagne flutes. Top with champagne.

Serves 4

LIME COOLER

10 dark green limes
4 cups/1 litre/1¾ pt water
1 cup/250 g/8 oz sugar

1 Finely grate limes into a bowl. Add measured water, cover and set aside for 1 hour.

2 Strain mixture through a fine sieve placed over a saucepan, pressing the rind to extract as much liquid as possible. Add sugar and stir over low heat until sugar dissolves.

3 Remove from the heat and allow the mixture to cool, then pour into a jug and refrigerate until required. Serve over ice.

Serves 6-8

RASPBERRY COOLER

500 g/1 lb fresh or thawed frozen raspberries
1 cup/250 mL/8 fl oz orange juice
4 tablespoons fresh lime juice
4 tablespoons sugar

1 Place all the ingredients in a blender or food processor; process until smooth. Strain through a fine sieve over a jug to remove seeds. Half fill four cocktail glasses with crushed ice, divide the mixture between them and serve at once.

Serves 4

TROPICAL PASSION

185 g/6 oz fresh or drained canned mango slices, chopped
½ cup/125 mL/4 fl oz peach liqueur
4 tablespoons cream (single)
8-12 ice cubes
2 cups/500 mL/16 fl oz lemonade

1 Place mango, liqueur and cream in a blender or food processor; process until smooth. Divide ice cubes between four large wine glasses, pour mango mixture over, top with lemonade, stir and serve.

Serves 4

Pineapple Rum Punch

CHARDONNAY PUNCH

**2 x 750 mL/1¼ pt bottles
  Chardonnay**
2 tablespoons maraschino
2 tablespoons curaçao
2 tablespoons cointreau
1 Granny Smith apple, sliced
8 strawberries, hulled

1 Pour both bottles of Chardonnay into a large punch bowl. Add the liquers and stir well.

2 Serve in punch bowl cups or wine glasses, adding a slice or two of apple and a strawberry to each.

Serves 8

LOVING CUP

**1 x 750 mL/1¼ pt bottle light red
  wine**
⅔ cup/170 mL/5½ fl oz curaçao
¾ cup/125 g/4 oz icing sugar
**rind of 1 lemon, pared in a long
  twist**
**rind of 1 orange, pared in a long
  twist**
**1 x 750 mL/1¼ pt bottle dry
  champagne or sparkling wine**
**250 g/8 oz sweet black grapes,
  skinned, halved and seeded**
crystallized violets (optional)
ice cubes

1 Mix the red wine, curacao, icing sugar and citrus rind twists in a large punch bowl. Refrigerate for 1 hour.

2 Stir in the champagne or sparkling wine, grapes and a handful of crystallized violets (if using). Add plenty of ice and serve at once.

Serves 10-12

BLACK VELVET

**5 cups/1.25 litres/2 pt Guinness,
  chilled**
**5 cups/1.25 litres/2 pt dry
  champagne, chilled**

Pour the Guinness and champagne simultaneously into a large jug. Serve at once, in tall glasses or tankards.

Serves 8

PINEAPPLE COOLER

crushed ice and ice cubes
**3 cups/750 mL/1¼ pt pineapple
  juice, chilled**
**1 x 750 mL/1¼ pt bottle dry white
  wine, chilled**
⅓ cup/60 g/2 oz icing sugar
**5 cups/1.25 litres/2 pt soda water,
  chilled**
**rind of 1 orange, pared in a long
  twist**
**rind of 1 lemon, pared in a long
  twist**
mint sprigs

1 Half fill a large jug with crushed ice. Pour in pineapple juice and white wine. Add icing sugar and stir until dissolved.

2 Top with soda water, stir again, and add twists of orange and lemon rind. Float mint sprigs on top.

3 Serve in tall glasses, adding an ice cube to each.

Serves 12-14

CHAMPAGNE CUP

**2 x 750 mL/1¼ pt bottles dry
  champagne**
⅓ cup/90 mL/3 fl oz brandy
⅓ cup/90 mL/3 fl oz curaçao
2 tablespoons lemon juice
**3 cups/750 mL/1¼ pt soda water,
  chilled**
2 tablespoons icing sugar
2 nectarines, sliced
250 g/8 oz raspberries, hulled
mint sprigs
crushed ice

1 Stand a punch bowl in a larger bowl of crushed ice. Mix champagne, brandy, curaçao and lemon juice in the punch bowl, then add soda water.

2 Stir in icing sugar gradually, taking care that the liquid does not spill over; it will be very effervescent.

3 Add nectarine slices, raspberries and mint sprigs. Serve at once, over crushed ice in champagne flutes.

Serves 14-16

SANGRIA

2 oranges, thinly sliced
2 lemons, thinly sliced
⅔ cup/170 mL/5½ fl oz brandy
block of ice
**1 x 750 mL/1¼ pt bottle red wine,
  chilled**
**2½ cups/625 mL/1 pt soda water,
  chilled**

1 Place orange and lemon slices in a bowl. Pour brandy over. Macerate for 1 hour in the refrigerator.

2 Put a block of ice into a large jug, add macerated fruit and brandy mixture and stir in wine.

3 Top with soda water. Serve at once, in wine glasses.

Serves 8-10

Cook's Tip: Lemonade may be used instead of soda water, if preferred, and a lime substituted for one of the lemons.

ROTHSCHILD CUP

250 g/8 oz strawberries, hulled
¾ cup/125 g/4 oz icing sugar
crushed ice
**1 x 750 mL/1¼ pt bottle dry
  champagne or sparkling wine**

1 Purée strawberries with icing sugar in a blender or food processor.

2 Half fill 10-12 tall glasses with crushed ice. Pour a little of the strawberry purée over the ice in each glass. Top with chilled champagne or sparkling wine, stir and serve at once.

Serves 10-12

From left, Loving Cup, Pineapple Cooler (in jug), Champagne Cup and Rothschild Cup

FLAVOURSOME FISH

Although fishermen have always appreciated the flavour of fish cooked over an open fire, it is only in relatively recent times that seafood has started to supersede meat on the barbecue grill. The reason for its growing popularity is not hard to find; from scallops to whole salmon, seafood remains succulent, tasty and tender when cooked with care over the coals.

◆ ◆ ◆

GRILLED TROUT WITH APPLE STUFFING

4 small trout, cleaned, with heads and tails intact
olive oil (see method)

APPLE STUFFING
30 g/1 oz butter
1 small onion, finely chopped
1 apple, peeled, cored and finely chopped
½ cup/30 g/1 oz fresh white breadcrumbs
1 teaspoon lemon juice
1 tablespoon finely chopped fresh mint
2 teaspoons finely chopped fresh parsley
freshly ground black pepper

1 To make stuffing, melt butter in a frying pan. Cook onion for 5 minutes or until soft and transparent. Tip into a bowl. Add apple, breadcrumbs, lemon juice, mint and parsley, with black pepper to taste. Mix well.

2 Fill the cavity in each trout with a quarter of the stuffing. Secure opening with toothpicks (cocktail sticks) and lightly brush outside of each trout with oil.

3 Cook on a lightly oiled barbecue grill over moderately hot coals for 5-8 minutes on each side, or until fish flakes when tested with the tip of a sharp knife.

Serves 4

MARINATED KING PRAWNS
Illustrated on page 77

20 uncooked king prawns, in shells

MARINADE
½ cup/125 mL/4 fl oz sunflower oil
2 tablespoons white wine vinegar
1 tablespoon soy sauce
2 tablespoons tomato paste (purée)
pinch chilli powder
1 small onion, finely chopped

SAUCE
⅔ cup/170 g/5½ oz mayonnaise
1 tablespoon tomato paste (purée)
pinch chilli powder
1 clove garlic, crushed

1 Make the marinade. Mix oil, vinegar, soy sauce, tomato paste (purée) and chilli powder in a bowl. Stir in chopped onion. Pour into a shallow dish large enough to hold all the prawns in a single layer.

2 Add prawns in their shells, turning to coat them in the marinade. Cover and marinate for 2 hours.

3 To make sauce, mix mayonnaise, tomato paste (purée), chilli powder and garlic in a bowl; beat well.

4 Drain prawns, discarding marinade. Cook on an oiled barbecue grill over moderately hot coals for 1 minute on each side. Serve at once, with sauce.

Serves 4

BACON AND PRAWN KEBABS

2 tablespoons Dijon mustard
2 cloves garlic, crushed
½ red pepper, cored, seeded and finely chopped
2 tablespoons finely chopped fresh dill
4 tablespoons olive oil
4 tablespoons lemon juice
freshly ground black pepper
20 large cooked prawns, shelled and deveined, tails left intact
8 rashers lean rindless bacon, cut into twenty 7.5 cm/3 in strips

1 Place mustard, garlic, red pepper, dill, oil and lemon juice in a shallow dish large enough to hold all the prawns in a single layer. Stir well and add black pepper to taste.

2 Add prawns, turning to coat them in the mixture. Cover and marinate for 30 minutes.

3 Drain prawns, reserving marinade. Wrap a strip of bacon around each prawn. Thread five bacon-wrapped prawns onto a metal skewer. Fill three more skewers in the same way.

4 Brush kebabs with reserved marinade. Cook on a lightly oiled barbecue grill over moderately hot coals for 2-3 minutes, turning at least twice, until bacon is crisp. Serve.

Serves 4

Grilled Trout with Apple Stuffing, Garlic and Herb Potato Rounds (page 58) and Bruschetta with Tomato and Olives (page 66)

BARBECUED WHOLE SALMON WITH LEMON NUT STUFFING

1 x 2.25 kg/4½ lb salmon, cleaned, with head and tail intact

STUFFING
30 g/1 oz butter
1 onion, finely chopped
1 stalk celery, finely chopped
2 lemons
4 cups/250 g/8 oz fresh wholemeal breadcrumbs
30 g/1 oz flaked almonds, finely chopped
salt
freshly ground black pepper

1 To make stuffing, melt butter in a small saucepan, add onion and celery and cook over moderately low heat for 5 minutes until onion is softened and transparent.

2 Using the fine side of a grater, grate the rind of both lemons into a bowl, taking care to avoid the pith. Stir in breadcrumbs, almonds and onion mixture, with salt and black pepper to taste.

3 Squeeze one lemon and add juice to stuffing. Mix well. Slice remaining lemon thinly, place on a plate, cover closely and set aside.

4 Fill cavity in salmon evenly with stuffing. Wrap fish loosely but securely in two layers of foil, then wrap a third piece of foil around the centre of the 'parcel' to support it and make a handle for easy transfer to, and removal from, the barbecue.

5 Place foil-wrapped fish on a barbecue grill over moderately hot coals. Cook until salmon flesh is tender and flakes easily when tested with the point of a sharp knife. The timing will depend on the temperature of the coals, the position of the grill and the type of barbecue used. As a guide, a fish cooked in this way in a kettle barbecue with the lid on will require 45-60 minutes.

6 Transfer salmon to a large platter. Fold back the foil to reveal the fish, garnish with the reserved lemon slices and serve at once.

Serves 10-12

HOT CHILLI PRAWNS WITH MANGO CREAM

1.5 kg/3 lb uncooked large prawns, peeled and deveined with tails left intact

CHILLI MARINADE
2 teaspoons crushed black peppercorns
2 tablespoons sweet chilli sauce
1 tablespoon soy sauce
1 clove garlic, crushed
¼ cup/60 mL/2 fl oz lemon juice

MANGO CREAM
1 mango, peeled, stoned and roughly chopped
3 tablespoons coconut milk (see Cook's Tip)

1 To make marinade, place crushed black peppercorns, chilli sauce, soy sauce, garlic and lemon juice in a bowl; mix to combine. Add prawns, toss to coat, cover and marinate for 1 hour. Toss several times during marinating.

2 To make mango cream, purée mango flesh with coconut milk in a blender or food processor until smooth. Scrape into a bowl and set aside.

3 Drain prawns, discarding marinade. Cook on a lightly oiled barbecue grill over moderately hot coals for 3-4 minutes or until prawns change colour. Serve at once, with mango cream.

Cook's Tip: Coconut milk is available from Asian food stores and some supermarkets in cans, as a long-life product in cartons and as a powder which is reconstituted with water. Once opened it has a short shelf life and should be used within a day or so. To make your own coconut milk, soak 500 g/1 lb desiccated coconut in 3 cups/750 mL/1¼ pt boiling water in a heatproof bowl. Set aside for 30 minutes. Press the mixture through a strainer set over a bowl, squeezing the coconut to extract as much liquid as possible.

Hot Chilli Prawns with Mango Cream

SPICY FISH STICKS

4 small white fish fillets
1 French bread stick, cut into 4
30 g/1 oz butter, softened
1 lettuce, shredded
1 tomato, sliced
4 tablespoons tartare sauce

MARINADE
1 tablespoon oil
2 tablespoons finely chopped
fresh coriander
2 tablespoons lemon juice
¼ teaspoon chilli powder
½ teaspoon ground cumin

1 To make marinade, place oil, coriander, lemon juice, chilli powder and cumin in a bowl; mix to combine. Place fish in a single layer in a shallow glass or ceramic dish and pour marinade over. Cover and marinate for 15 minutes, turning fish fillets once.

2 Cut each piece of bread stick in half horizontally; toast on a barbecue grill over moderately hot coals. Spread with butter, then top bottom halves of each piece of toasted French bread with lettuce. Add tomato slices.

Spicy Fish Sticks, Vegetable Kebabs with Mustard Sauce (page 38)

3 Cook fish fillets on lightly oiled barbecue grill for 2 minutes each side, or until flesh flakes easily when tested with the tip of a sharp knife.

4 Add fish fillets and tartare sauce to each prepared bread stick slice and top with lids. Serve at once.

Serves 4

BARBECUED MACKEREL

**4 small mackerel, cleaned, with
  heads and tails intact**
1 clove garlic, crushed
⅔ cup/170 mL/5½ fl oz olive oil
4 tablespoons lemon juice
1 teaspoon salt
freshly ground black pepper
**2 tablespoons chopped fresh
  thyme**

GOOSEBERRY SAUCE
**375 g/12 oz gooseberries, topped
  and tailed**
2 tablespoons water
**finely grated rind and juice of
  1 lemon**
15 g/½ oz butter
1 teaspoon caster sugar

1   Slash the skin on both sides of
each mackerel at 5 cm/2 in intervals.
Rub garlic into the slashes.

2   Place olive oil, lemon juice and
salt in a shallow dish large enough to
hold all the fish in a single layer. Stir
in black pepper to taste. Add fish to
the dish, spoon marinade over and
sprinkle with thyme. Cover the dish
and marinate the mackerel for
45 minutes, turning once.

3   Make gooseberry sauce. Place
gooseberries and measured water in
a saucepan. Cover and cook over
low heat for about 10 minutes, until
fruit is soft. Purée in a blender or food
processor, then press through a sieve
and return to the clean pan. Stir in
lemon rind, juice, butter and sugar.
Heat, stirring, until butter melts.

4   Drain mackerel, reserving
marinade. Place in an oiled hinged
grill. Cook over moderately hot coals
for 5-7 minutes each side. Brush
frequently with the reserved
marinade, but take care, as the oil
will cause the fire to flare. Protect
your hand with a barbecue mitt, and
be ready to move the hinged grill
away from the flames if necessary.
Serve the mackerel with the
gooseberry sauce.

Serves 4

SWORDFISH WITH TOMATO SAUCE

4 swordfish steaks

SAUCE
2 tablespoons sunflower oil
1 large onion, chopped
2 cloves garlic, crushed
1 red chilli, seeded and chopped
**2 large tomatoes, peeled and
  roughly chopped**
**2 tablespoons tomato paste
  (purée)**
5 tablespoons water
2 tablespoons red wine vinegar
1 teaspoon lemon juice
pinch sugar
freshly ground black pepper
2 tablespoons pitted black olives

1   To make the sauce, heat the oil in
a saucepan, add the onion and garlic
and cook over moderate heat for
5 minutes until softened and
transparent.

2   Add the chilli and tomatoes and
simmer for 10 minutes, then stir in
the tomato paste (purée), measured
water, vinegar, lemon juice and
sugar. Add black pepper to taste.
Simmer for 15 minutes, then stir in
the black olives.

3   Prepare four squares of foil, each
large enough to comfortably enclose
a swordfish steak. Place the foil
squares shiny side up, centre a
swordfish steak on each, and divide
the sauce between them, spooning it
over the fish. Close the parcels
loosely but securely. If necessary,
wrap in a second layer of foil.

4   Cook the foil packages on a
barbecue grill over moderately hot
coals for 20 minutes or until the fish
is tender and flakes easily when
tested with the point of a sharp knife.
Transfer each parcel to a plate, open
the foil to reveal the sauce-coated
fish, and serve.

Serves 4

SALMON CUTLETS WITH PINEAPPLE SALSA

4 salmon cutlets, about 2.5 cm/1 in thick

PINEAPPLE SALSA
250 g/8 oz fresh pineapple, roughly chopped, or 1 x 375 g/12 oz can crushed pineapple in natural juice
2 spring onions, finely chopped
1 red chilli, seeded and finely chopped
1 tablespoon lemon juice
2 tablespoons finely chopped fresh mint

1   Make salsa by placing pineapple, spring onions, chilli, lemon juice and mint in a blender or food processor; process briefly to combine (the sauce should retain some texture). Scrape into a small bowl. Garnish, if liked, with a mint sprig.

2   Cook salmon cutlets on a lightly oiled barbecue grill over moderately hot coals for 3-5 minutes each side, or until flesh flakes easily when tested with the point of a sharp knife. Serve at once, with the salsa. Lightly cooked green asparagus makes a delicious accompaniment.

Serves 4

Cook's Tip: If preferred, serve the salmon cutlets with a savoury butter.

LIME AND PARSLEY BUTTER
Combine 125 g/4 oz softened butter with 2 tablespoons grated lime rind and 2 tablespoons finely chopped fresh parsley. Add salt and black pepper to taste. Form the mixture into a roll, wrap in foil and chill until firm. To serve, cut in 8 rounds. Place 2 rounds on each grilled salmon cutlet. Garnish with twists of lime.

TOMATO BUTTER
Combine 125 g/4 oz softened butter with 3 tablespoons tomato paste (purée). Beat with a wooden spoon until very well mixed, then beat in a dash of Tabasco sauce. Form into a roll, chill and use as suggested above.

Salmon Cutlets with Pineapple Salsa

SALAD DAYS

*Complement the main attraction with a selection of stunning salads.
Dressed green leaves are appropriate for all types of grilled food,
while a warm bean and vegetable salad would be perfect with country
pork sausages or frankfurters. Serve a refreshing orange or
carrot salad with barbecued chicken, and a rice salad inspired by
the Orient with seafood kebabs. Best of all, mix and match
to add colour and flavour to your barbecue buffet.*

♦ ◆ ♦

BOW PASTA SALAD

**250 g/8 oz dried bow pasta
1 quantity hot Sun-dried Tomato
Sauce (page 62)
⅔ cup/170 ml/5½ fl oz chicken
stock
1 leek, finely sliced
1 zucchini (courgette), cut into
thin strips
2 tablespoons pine nuts, toasted
2 tablespoons finely chopped
fresh basil
2 tablespoons finely chopped
fresh parsley**

1   Cook pasta in boiling water in a
saucepan, following packet directions.
Drain well and transfer to a bowl. Add
sauce, toss well and set pasta aside
to cool.

2   Place stock and leek in a frying
pan and cook over moderate heat for
5 minutes or until leek softens. Add
zucchini (courgette) and cook for
1 minute more. Drain, tip into a bowl
and set aside to cool.

3   Add zucchini (courgette) mixture,
pine nuts, basil and parsley to pasta.
Toss to combine. Cover salad and
chill until required.

Serves 4

WARM BEAN AND VEGETABLE SALAD

Illustrated on page 51

**1 red pepper
1 green pepper
1 red onion, finely chopped
2 spring onions, finely chopped
3 tomatoes, peeled and finely diced
1 clove garlic, crushed
750 g/1½ lb canned mixed beans,
drained
1 red chilli, seeded and finely
chopped
2 tablespoons red wine vinegar
1 tablespoon sunflower oil
3 tablespoons finely chopped
fresh coriander
freshly ground black pepper**

1   Place red and green pepper under
a hot grill or on an oiled barbecue grill
over moderately hot coals until skin
blisters and chars. Transfer to a
paper or plastic food bag. When cool
enough to handle, remove skin, cut
peppers into strips and place in a
large bowl.

2   Add red onion, spring onions,
tomatoes, garlic, beans, chilli and
vinegar. Toss to combine.

3   Heat oil in a large frying pan on
barbecue grill. Add vegetable mixture.
Cook, stirring, for 4-5 minutes or until
just warmed. Stir in coriander, with
black pepper to taste. Serve.

Serves 6

CLASSIC GREEN SALAD WITH CHIFFONADE DRESSING

**1 large lettuce, separated into
leaves, or a selection of green
leaves, washed and dried**

DRESSING
**2 hard-boiled eggs, finely chopped
½ small red pepper, cored, seeded
and finely chopped
1 tablespoon finely chopped
shallot or spring onion
2 tablespoons finely chopped fresh
parsley
2 tablespoons white wine vinegar
3 tablespoons olive oil
3 tablespoons sunflower oil
salt
freshly ground black pepper**

1   To make the dressing, mix the
hard-boiled eggs, red pepper and
shallot or spring onion in a salad
bowl. Add the parsley and vinegar
and mix well. Gradually whisk in the
oils until the dressing is well
combined. Whisk in salt and pepper
to taste.

2   Add the lettuce leaves to the bowl
and toss to coat well. Serve at once.

Serves 4

*Classic Green Salad with Chiffonade
Dressing*

POTATO, BACON AND APPLE SALAD

500 g/1 lb salad potatoes
salt
4 rashers lean rindless bacon,
  diced
1 teaspoon soft light brown sugar
1 teaspoon Dijon mustard
1 tablespoon cider vinegar
4 tablespoons olive oil
freshly ground black pepper
2 red eating apples
2 tablespoons lemon juice
2 spring onions, finely chopped
lemon slices to garnish

1   Cook potatoes in their jackets in a saucepan of lightly salted boiling water until just tender.

2   Heat bacon in a saucepan until the fat runs. Fry until crisp, then remove with a slotted spoon and drain on absorbent kitchen paper.

3   Add sugar, mustard and vinegar to bacon fat remaining in pan. Stir over moderate heat until hot, then tip into a heatproof bowl and whisk in oil. Add black pepper to taste.

4   Drain potatoes. When cool enough to handle, remove skins and cut flesh into cubes. Place in a large bowl. Pour over dressing, toss gently and set aside until cold.

5   Slice apples and toss in lemon juice to prevent discoloration. Add spring onions and bacon to potato mixture and pile in the centre of a square serving dish. Drain apple slices and arrange on opposite sides of dish. Garnish with lemon slices.

Serves 4

MIXED LEAVES WITH AVOCADO, SUN-DRIED TOMATOES AND FETA

a selection of mixed lettuce leaves,
  washed and dried
185 g/6 oz feta cheese, cubed
2 ripe avocados, halved, stoned
  and peeled
4 tablespoons lemon juice
3 tablespoons olive oil
6 drained sun-dried tomatoes in
  oil, sliced
pinch soft light brown sugar

1   Arrange lettuce leaves in a salad bowl. Add feta cubes and toss lightly. Slice avocados thinly into a separate bowl, toss lightly in lemon juice to prevent discoloration and set aside.

2   Heat olive oil in a small frying pan, add sun-dried tomatoes and fry for 2 minutes. Using a slotted spoon, add tomatoes to salad bowl.

3   Drain avocados and add to salad, pouring lemon juice into frying pan. Add sugar. Heat, stirring, until mixture bubbles, then pour over salad, toss quickly and serve at once.

Serves 6

Cook's Tip: Any flavoursome cheese may be used in this salad. Try thin slices of a Bavarian smoked cheese or crumble in Roquefort.

MARINATED MUSHROOM SALAD
Illustrated on pages 28-29

4 tablespoons olive oil
2 cloves garlic, crushed
750 g/1½ lb small button
  mushrooms, trimmed
2 tablespoons red wine vinegar
1 tablespoon lemon juice
3 tablespoons chicken stock
1 tablespoon chopped fresh basil
2 tablespoons chopped fresh
  parsley

1   Heat olive oil in a frying pan and cook garlic and mushrooms for 2-3 minutes. Reduce heat, stir in vinegar, lemon juice and stock, then simmer for 1 minute.

2   Stir in basil and parsley. Transfer to a bowl and set aside. When cool, cover and refrigerate until required.

Serves 8-10

Potato, Bacon and Apple Salad

Mixed Pepper Salad

MIXED PEPPER SALAD

1 green pepper, sliced in strips
1 red pepper, sliced in strips
2 tomatoes, peeled, seeded and
** sliced in strips**
½ mild onion, thinly sliced
60 g/2 oz cooked ham, cut in strips

DRESSING
2 tablespoons red wine vinegar
pinch caster sugar
1 teaspoon garlic and red pepper
** mustard**
5 tablespoons olive oil
salt
freshly ground black pepper

1 Make dressing by whisking vinegar, sugar and mustard together in a small bowl, then whisking in oil. Add salt and pepper to taste, whisk again and set aside.

2 Mix peppers, tomatoes and onion in a large shallow bowl. Pour dressing over, toss thoroughly, cover and marinate for 1 hour.

3 About 15 minutes before serving, add ham strips and toss again.

Serves 4

WATERMELON AND NECTARINE SALAD

1 large wedge watermelon, about
** 750 g/1½ lb**
2 nectarines, thinly sliced

DRESSING
2 tablespoons red wine vinegar or
** raspberry vinegar**
1 tablespoon orange juice
½ teaspoon soy sauce
4 tablespoons light olive oil

1 Remove skin from watermelon, then slice wedge to make triangles, removing any seeds. Arrange around the rim of a platter, then add an inner circle of nectarine slices. Continue adding alternate circles of watermelon and nectarine until the platter is filled.

2 Make dressing by mixing vinegar, orange juice and soy sauce in a bowl, then whisking in oil.

3 Spoon dressing over salad, cover and allow to stand for at least 1 hour to allow flavours to develop.

Serves 6

BLUE CHEESE CAESAR SALAD

Illustrated on pages 48-49

2 rashers rindless streaky bacon, chopped
1 cos or iceberg lettuce, separated into leaves, washed and dried
60 g/2 oz pine nuts, toasted
125 g/4 oz Parmesan cheese, grated

CROÛTONS
⅓ cup/90 mL/3 fl oz olive oil
2 slices bread, crusts removed, cut into 1 cm/½ in cubes

BLUE CHEESE DRESSING
90 g/3 oz Stilton cheese
2 tablespoons natural yogurt
2 tablespoons sour cream
⅓ cup/90 mL/3 fl oz thickened cream (double)
2 tablespoons lemon juice
freshly ground black pepper

1 To make croûtons, heat oil in a frying pan, add bread cubes and fry over moderate heat, tossing frequently, for 1-2 minutes or until golden on all sides. Using a slotted spoon, remove the croûtons from the pan and drain thoroughly on absorbent kitchen paper.

2 Heat bacon in a frying pan until the fat runs, then fry over moderate heat for 3-4 minutes or until crisp. Drain on absorbent kitchen paper.

3 To make dressing, crumble Stilton into a blender or food processor. Add yogurt, sour cream, thickened (double) cream, lemon juice and black pepper to taste. Process until smooth and creamy.

4 Tear the lettuce into bite-sized pieces and place in a serving bowl. Add bacon, croûtons and pine nuts. Pour dressing over and toss. Sprinkle with Parmesan cheese and serve immediately.

Serves 8

ORANGE AND OLIVE SALAD

4 oranges
1 head endive (frisée), washed, dried and torn into bite-sized pieces
12 pitted black olives

DRESSING
2 tablespoons orange juice
2 tablespoons lemon juice
1 clove garlic, crushed
5 tablespoons olive oil
salt
freshly ground black pepper

1 Make dressing by mixing orange juice, lemon juice and garlic in a small bowl or jug. Whisk in olive oil, then add salt and pepper to taste.

2 Peel oranges, taking care to remove all the pith. Slice thinly and place in a shallow bowl. Add the dressing, toss lightly, then cover and refrigerate for 1 hour.

3 Place endive (frisée) in a large shallow salad bowl. Drain orange slices, reserving dressing. Add half the dressing to the endive (frisée) and toss lightly, then spread out to make an even bed for the orange slices.

4 Arrange orange slices in an overlapping circle on the endive (frisée) as illustrated opposite. Dot with black olives. Drizzle remaining dressing over orange slices and serve at once.

Serves 4

Cook's Tips: As an alternative, try radicchio with pink grapefruit. Use grapefruit juice in place of the orange juice in the main recipe. For a more substantial salad – the famous Ensalada Sevillana – add 1 sliced red pepper and 1 sliced red onion to the Orange and Olive Salad.

Orange and Olive Salad

TOMATO AND MOZZARELLA SALAD

500 g/1 lb beefsteak tomatoes,
** sliced**
salt
freshly ground black pepper
3 tablespoons extra virgin olive oil
250 g/8 oz fresh mozzarella cheese
** (see Cook's Tips)**
1 tablespoon chopped fresh basil
6-8 black olives
basil sprig to garnish

1   Arrange tomato slices in concentric circles on a large platter. Sprinkle with salt and black pepper, then drizzle with olive oil.

2   Drain mozzarella. Slice lengthwise into three thick slices and arrange these in the centre of the salad as illustrated opposite.

3   Sprinkle the salad with the chopped basil and dot with the olives. Garnish with a basil sprig and serve.

Serves 4

Cook's Tips: Use fresh mozzarella, preferably made from buffalo milk and packed in whey. Olive oil is traditionally the only dressing, but a little red wine vinegar may be added.

PICKLED VEGETABLE SALAD
Illustrated on pages 38-39

3 cups/750 mL/1¼ pt distilled
** (white) vinegar**
2 tablespoons sugar
2 teaspoons salt
1 large cucumber, peeled, seeded
** and cubed**
1 small cauliflower, cut into small
** florets**
2 large carrots, sliced
1 head broccoli, cut into small
** florets**
1 red pepper, diced
1 green pepper, diced
440 g/14 oz can baby corn cobs,
** drained**
2 cloves garlic, chopped
1 large onion, chopped
2 dried red chillies, seeded and
** finely chopped**
3 tablespoons sunflower oil
1 tablespoon sesame seeds,
** roasted**

1   Place vinegar, sugar and salt in a large saucepan. Bring to the boil, then add cucumber, cauliflower, carrots, broccoli, diced red and green pepper and baby corn cobs. Cook for 1 minute, then remove the pan from the heat and set aside to cool.

2   Place garlic, onion and chillies in a blender or food processor; process to a smooth paste. Heat oil in a large saucepan, add garlic paste and cook for 2-3 minutes, then add vegetable and vinegar mixture. Cook for 1 minute more. Stir in sesame seeds and serve at once, or spoon into sterilized jars and seal. When cold, store in the refrigerator for up to two weeks.

Serves 8

Cook's Tip: If preferred, the garlic and chillies may be reduced to a paste in a mortar. Use a pestle to grind them finely, adding a little oil if liked. Fry the onion in the remaining oil before adding the garlic paste.

CARROT AND CITRUS SALAD

3 carrots
2 oranges
2 tablespoons sultanas
2 tablespoons red wine vinegar
1 tablespoon lemon juice
6 tablespoons sunflower oil
salt
freshly ground black pepper

1   Grate carrots finely into a bowl. Peel oranges, taking care to remove all the pith. Working over the bowl of carrots to catch any juice, cut oranges into segments.

2   Add orange segments to bowl with sultanas.

3   Whisk vinegar, lemon juice and oil together in a small jug or bowl. Add salt and pepper to taste, then pour over salad. Toss well. Cover and allow to stand for at least 1 hour before serving.

Serves 4-6

ORIENTAL RICE SALAD
Illustrated on pages 38-39

125 g/4 oz long grain white rice
125 g/4 oz long grain brown rice
125 g/4 oz wild rice
1 tablespoon sunflower oil
2 cloves garlic, crushed
4 spring onions, chopped
125 g/4 oz snow peas (mangetout),
** topped and tailed**
90 g/3 oz unsalted cashews,
** toasted**

SESAME DRESSING
3 tablespoons brown (malt)
** vinegar**
2 teaspoons soy sauce
1 teaspoon sesame oil
½ teaspoon sugar

1   Cook white, brown and wild rice separately in three saucepans of boiling water, following packet directions in each case. Drain and set aside to cool.

2   Heat oil in a frying pan. Cook garlic and spring onions over moderate heat for 3-4 minutes or until onions soften. Add snow peas (mangetout) and cashews; cook for 3-4 minutes longer or until snow peas are just tender. Remove from heat and set aside to cool.

3   To make dressing, combine vinegar, soy sauce, oil and sugar in a screwtop jar, close the lid tightly and shake to combine.

4   Mix white, brown and wild rice in a large salad bowl. Add snow pea mixture and toss to distribute all ingredients evenly. Pour dressing over, toss again to combine, then cover and chill until required.

Serves 8

Tomato and Mozzarella Salad

FAST FOOD

These are the family favourites: the quick suppers to feed starving teenagers; the casual cookouts when everyone brings a bottle and a contribution to the salad table. In this chapter you'll find hot dogs and hamburgers, including a vegetarian choice, plus steak sandwiches, filled pitta pockets and kebabs with every type of filling, from fish to curried chicken, meat and mushrooms.

♦ ◆ ♦

BEST EVER HAMBURGERS

**10 wholemeal rolls or sesame
  buns, split in half
lettuce leaves
tomato slices
cheese slices
pickled beetroot
onion rings
gherkins
tomato ketchup (sauce)
mustard
mayonnaise**

MEAT PATTIES
**1 kg/2 lb minced beef
1 onion, finely chopped
1 small carrot, grated
1 cup/60 g/2 oz fresh white
  breadcrumbs
1 tablespoon Worcestershire
  sauce
1 tablespoon tomato ketchup
  (sauce)
dash Tabasco (hot chilli sauce)
  or to taste
2 tablespoons finely chopped
  fresh parsley
freshly ground black pepper**

1 Make patties. Mix minced beef, onion, carrot and breadcrumbs in a large bowl. Add Worcestershire sauce and tomato ketchup (sauce), Tabasco (hot chilli sauce), parsley and pepper. Using clean hands, mix to combine.

2 If you prefer to make the pattie mixture in a food processor, crumb the bread (2 slices) in the processor and tip into a bowl. Chop onion and grate carrot in processor, then add remaining ingredients and process briefly until combined. Add to breadcrumbs and mix thoroughly.

3 Shape mixture into ten patties, either in a hamburger press or by using clean wet hands. Place patties on a baking sheet, cover closely and refrigerate until required.

4 Cook on a lightly oiled barbecue grill over hot coals for 4-5 minutes each side, or until cooked to your liking, pressing patties down with a spatula during grilling. Toast rolls or buns on barbecue.

5 Have ready any or all of the suggested fillings so that each guest can assemble his or her version of the Best Ever Hamburger.

Serves 10

Best Ever Hamburgers

PIQUANT BURGERS

500 g/1 lb minced beef
2 tablespoons chopped fresh
  parsley
2 tablespoons chopped mild onion
2 tablespoons rinsed capers,
  chopped if large
2 tablespoons Dijon mustard
1 beefsteak tomato, chopped
6 sun-dried tomatoes in oil,
  drained and chopped
1 egg, beaten
freshly ground black pepper
½ cup/60 g/2 oz grated mozzarella
  cheese

1 Mix minced beef, parsley, onion,
capers, mustard, beefsteak tomato
and sun-dried tomatoes in a bowl.
Mix well, using clean hands, then
work in sufficient egg to bind the
mixture, with black pepper to taste.

2 Using clean hands, divide mixture
into eight equal portions. Flatten each
slightly. Make an indentation in four
of the patties and fill with a quarter of
the mozzarella. Place remaining
patties on top to make four
'sandwiches'. Seal well.

3 Cook burgers on an oiled
barbecue grill over hot coals for 4-5
minutes each side, turning once.

Serves 4

BEAN BURGERS

1 red pepper, finely chopped
1 cup/250 g/8 oz mashed potato
440 g/14 oz can butter beans,
  drained and mashed
1 small onion, very finely chopped
4 sun-dried tomatoes in oil,
  drained and finely chopped
½ cup/30 g/1 oz wholemeal
  breadcrumbs, plus extra for
  coating
1 egg, beaten with 2 tablespoons
  milk
1 tablespoon sesame seeds
oil for brushing

1 Mix pepper, potato, butter beans,
onion, sun-dried tomatoes and
breadcrumbs in a bowl. Using wet
hands, shape into 4 generous patties.
Dip into egg mixture and coat in
breadcrumbs and sesame seeds.
Cover and chill for 1 hour. Cook as
for Vegetable Burgers opposite.

Serves 4

VEGETABLE BURGERS

**10 wholemeal rolls or sesame
  buns, split in half**
**10 lettuce leaves, washed and
  dried**
**1 quantity Spicy Tomato Sauce
  (page 62)**

PATTIES
500 g/1 lb broccoli, chopped
**500 g/1 lb zucchini (courgettes),
  chopped**
250 g/8 oz carrots, chopped
2 onions, finely chopped
2 cloves garlic, crushed
**3 tablespoons chopped fresh
  parsley**
**1½ cups/185 g/6 oz dried
  breadcrumbs**
½ cup/60 g/2 oz plain flour
freshly ground black pepper

1 To make patties, boil, steam or
microwave broccoli, zucchini
(courgettes) and carrots until tender.
Drain, rinse under cold running water,
drain again and pat dry.

2 Purée cooked vegetables with
onions, garlic and parsley in a
blender or food processor until
smooth. Transfer mixture to a mixing
bowl and add breadcrumbs and flour,
with black pepper to taste. Mix to
combine, cover and refrigerate for
30 minutes.

3 Using clean wet hands, shape
mixture into ten patties. Place on a
baking sheet lined with nonstick
baking paper, cover and refrigerate
until required.

4 Cook patties on a lightly oiled
barbecue plate (griddle) or in a
hinged grill for 3-4 minutes each side.
Toast rolls or buns on barbecue, then
fill each roll or bun with a lettuce leaf,
a pattie and a generous spoonful of
sauce. Serve at once.

Serves 10

*Barbecue Chips (page 57), Marinated
Mushroom Salad (page 20), Vegetable
Burgers*

SMOKY DOGS

8 large frankfurters (see Cook's Tip)
8 hot dog rolls
¼ cup/60 g/2 oz butter, softened
1 clove garlic, crushed or 1 spring onion, finely chopped
1 tablespoon finely chopped parsley
3 tablespoons tomato ketchup (sauce)
1 tablespoon mild American-style mustard

1   Using a sharp knife, cut diagonal slashes in each frankfurter, about 5 mm/¼ in deep.

2   Cut hot dog rolls in half lengthwise. In a small bowl, mix butter with garlic or spring onion and parsley. Spread mixture on cut sides of rolls.

3   In a separate bowl, mix tomato ketchup (sauce) with mustard.

4   Cook frankfurters on an oiled barbecue grill over hot coals for about 5 minutes, turning occasionally and brushing frequently with the mustard mixture.

5   Toast hot dog rolls, buttered side down, on barbecue, fill with frankfurters and serve with sauce.

Serves 8

Cook's Tip: Choose loose or vacuum-packed frankfurters for this recipe; canned frankfurters are not sufficiently firm.

SAUSAGE PITTA ROLLS

8 pork sausages
8 no-need-to-soak dried apricots
4 rashers lean rindless bacon, halved
8 small pitta breads
4 lettuce leaves, washed and dried
4 spring onions, finely chopped
2 carrots, grated

1   Precook sausages. Place them in a saucepan with water to cover, bring to the boil, then lower the heat and simmer for 5 minutes. Drain and set aside until cold. Alternatively, prick sausages all over and microwave on High for 10 minutes. Set aside.

2   If not grilling sausages immediately, cover and place in the refrigerator.

3   Make a slit in the side of each sausage and insert a dried apricot. 'Bandage' the sausage with a strip of bacon. Thread the sausages on two metal skewers.

4   Cook on an oiled barbecue grill over hot coals for about 15 minutes, turning several times, until bacon is crisp and sausages are cooked through.

5   Slit pittas and open up pockets. Warm on barbecue grill. Add a little lettuce, spring onions and grated carrot to each. Slide sausages off skewers and place one sausage in each filled pitta pocket. Serve.

Serves 8

HAWAIIAN CHEESE PATTIES

625 g/1¼ lb minced beef
1 tablespoon barbecue sauce
2 tablespoons tomato ketchup (sauce)
1 small onion, finely chopped
60 g/2 oz tasty cheese (mature Cheddar), grated
125 g/4 oz drained canned crushed pineapple

1   Mix minced beef, barbecue sauce, tomato ketchup (sauce) and onion in a bowl. Shape mixture into eight flat patties, either in a hamburger press or by using clean wet hands.

2   Top four patties with cheese and pineapple, then place remaining patties on top to make four 'sandwiches'. Carefully mould edges of patties together so that filling is completely sealed.

3   Cook filled patties on an oiled barbecue grill over hot coals for 4-5 minutes each side. Serve solo, with a selection of salads, or in sesame buns, with lettuce.

Serves 4

BARBECUED STEAK SANDWICHES

6 lean rump steaks, about 1 cm/½ in thick
3 onions, thinly sliced
12 thick slices wholemeal or granary bread
olive oil
6 lettuce leaves

WINE AND GINGER MARINADE
1 cup/250 mL/8 fl oz red wine
½ cup/125 mL/4 fl oz olive oil
1 clove garlic, crushed
2 teaspoons grated fresh root ginger

1   To make marinade, place red wine, oil, garlic and ginger in a shallow dish large enough to hold the steaks in a single layer. Mix well.

2   Add steaks to dish, turning to coat in marinade. Cover and marinate at room temperature for 2-3 hours or overnight in the refrigerator.

3   Cook onions on a lightly oiled barbecue plate (griddle) or in a lightly oiled frying pan on the barbecue grill for 10-15 minutes or until golden.

4   Drain steaks, discarding marinade. Cook on a lightly oiled barbecue grill over hot coals for 3-5 minutes each side or until cooked to your liking.

5   Lightly brush bread slices with oil; toast lightly on barbecue grill. Make up sandwiches, using lettuce, steak and onions as filling. Place on individual plates. Garnish with red pepper strips and fresh coriander, if liked.

Serves 6

Barbecued Steak Sandwiches

FALAFELS

Illustrated on page 42

220 g/7 oz chickpeas, soaked
  overnight in water to cover
90 g/3 oz burghul (cracked wheat)
½ cup/125 mL/4 fl oz water
2 cloves garlic, crushed
½ cup/30 g/1 oz fresh white
  breadcrumbs
1 egg, lightly beaten
1 tablespoon lemon juice
2 tablespoons chopped fresh
  coriander
½ teaspoon garam masala
¼ teaspoon turmeric
1 small red chilli, seeded and
  finely chopped
freshly ground black pepper
oil for shallow frying

1 Drain chickpeas, rinse under cold water and drain again. Tip into a large saucepan, add water to cover and bring to the boil. Lower the heat and simmer for 35-40 minutes or until chickpeas are cooked but still firm. Drain and set aside.

2 Place burghul (cracked wheat) in a bowl, add measured water and set aside to soak for 15 minutes. Strain the burgul, pressing it against the sides of the strainer to remove as much liquid as possible. Set burghul aside.

3 Process chickpeas in a blender or food processor until smooth, then add garlic, breadcrumbs, egg, lemon juice, coriander, garam masala, turmeric and chilli. Process again until combined. Scrape mixture into a bowl, add burgul with plenty of black pepper and mix well. Cover and chill for 1 hour.

4 Shape chickpea mixture into small oval patties (falafels). Arrange on a baking sheet lined with non-stick paper and chill for 30 minutes more.

5 Fry falafels in hot oil in a frying pan for 4-5 minutes or until golden. Drain on absorbent kitchen paper, then thread onto metal or soaked wooden skewers. Place on a lightly oiled barbecue grill over hot coals for 4-5 minutes or until heated through. Serve with Minted Yogurt (see page 62).

Makes 15

PITTA POCKETS WITH GRILLED RUMP STEAK

1 kg/2 lb rump steak, about
　3 cm/1¼ in thick, trimmed
6 large white pitta breads
3 tablespoons chopped fresh
　coriander

MARINADE
2 cloves garlic, crushed
⅓ cup/90 ml/3 fl oz red wine
¼ cup/60 ml/2 fl oz olive oil
1 teaspoon crushed black
　peppercorns

CORIANDER BUTTER SAUCE
125 g/4 oz butter
2 cloves garlic, chopped
2 egg yolks
1 tablespoon lemon juice
2 tablespoons chopped fresh
　coriander
1 tablespoon chopped fresh
　parsley

1　Make marinade by combining all
the ingredients in a shallow dish large
enough to hold the pieces of rump
steak. Mix well, add steak and turn to
coat thoroughly. Cover the dish and
marinate the steak for 1 hour.

2　Drain steak, discarding marinade.
Cook on an oiled barbecue grill over
hot coals for 7-8 minutes each side or
until cooked to your liking. Transfer to
a platter and keep warm on the edge
of the grill.

3　Make sauce. Heat butter in a
small saucepan until it bubbles. Place
garlic, egg yolks, lemon juice,
coriander and parsley in a blender or
food processor; process until smooth.
With the motor running, add bubbling
hot butter slowly through the feeder
tube. Continue to process sauce for
1 minute. Pour sauce into a bowl
and set aside to cool for 5 minutes.

4　Slice pitta breads in half and open
each half to make a pocket. Slice
steak diagonally across the grain and
arrange with coriander in pitta
pockets. Place two filled pockets on
each of 6 plates.

5　Whisk sauce vigorously for 30
seconds, spoon over meat in pockets
and serve at once. Garnish each
portion with a twist of lemon and a
knot of spring onion green, if liked.

Serves 6

PAUPIETTES

200 g/6½ oz feta cheese
90 g/3 oz Parmesan cheese, grated
3 cloves garlic, crushed
2 tablespoons chopped fresh
　parsley
3 spring onions, chopped
110 g/3½ oz cooked ham, roughly
　chopped
8 veal escalopes, pounded until
　thin

1　Place feta cheese, Parmesan,
garlic, parsley, spring onions and
ham in a food processor; process
to a rough paste.

2　Spread each veal escalope with
the cheese mixture, roll up and
secure with toothpicks (cocktail
sticks).

3　Cook paupiettes on a lightly oiled
barbecue plate (griddle) over
moderately hot coals until browned
and cooked through. Serve at once.

Serves 4

*Pitta Pockets with Grilled Rump Steak
(main picture), Paupiettes*

CURRIED CHICKEN KEBABS

750 g/1½ lb skinless chicken breast fillets, cut into 2.5 cm/1 in cubes

LIME CURRY GLAZE
1 cup/315 g/10 oz lime marmalade
2 tablespoons Dijon mustard
2 teaspoons curry powder
1 tablespoon fresh lime juice

1 To make glaze, place marmalade, mustard, curry powder and lime juice in a small saucepan. Cook, stirring, over moderate heat for 3 minutes or until ingredients combine to make a smooth sauce. Set aside to cool.

2 Thread chicken cubes onto 12 lightly oiled metal skewers. Place skewers in a shallow glass or ceramic dish large enough to hold them in a single layer. Spoon glaze mixture over, cover dish and marinate at room temperature for 1 hour.

3 Drain kebabs, reserving remaining glaze. Cook on lightly oiled barbecue grill over hot coals for 8-10 minutes or until cooked, turning frequently and brushing chicken occasionally with reserved glaze.

Serves 6

Cook's Tip: Use turkey fillet for a delicious change.

SEAFOOD KEBABS

1 salmon fillet, cut into eight 2 cm/¾ in cubes
8 scallops, cleaned
8 large uncooked prawns, shelled and deveined, tails left intact
1 large white fish fillet, cut into eight 2 cm/¾ in cubes
8 mussels, removed from shells

CHILLI LIME GLAZE
¼ cup/60 mL/2 fl oz olive oil
2 red chillies, seeded and finely chopped
1 clove garlic, crushed
¼ cup/60 mL/2 fl oz fresh lime juice

1 Lightly oil eight metal kebab skewers. Thread a skewer with a cube of salmon, a scallop, a prawn, a piece of white fish and a mussel. Repeat with remaining seafood and skewers.

2 To make glaze, place oil, chillies, garlic and lime juice in a small bowl; mix to combine.

3 Brush kebabs with glaze. Cook on a lightly oiled barbecue grill over moderately hot coals, turning frequently and brushing with any remaining glaze, for 3-4 minutes or until seafood changes colour and is cooked through. Serve at once.

Serves 4

AVOCADO AND PRAWN SKEWERS
Illustrated on pages 36-37

2 avocados, halved, stoned, peeled and cut into cubes
3 tablespoons lemon juice
20 cooked large prawns, shelled and deveined, tails left intact
10 cherry tomatoes, halved
oil for greasing

TOMATO DIPPING SAUCE
½ cup/125 mL/4 fl oz sour cream
½ cup/125 g/4 oz mayonnaise
2 tablespoons tomato ketchup (sauce)
2 teaspoons Worcestershire sauce

1 Lightly oil 10 wooden skewers. Place avocado cubes in a bowl. Pour lemon juice over and toss cubes lightly to coat.

2 Drain avocado cubes. Thread two prawns, three avocado cubes and two tomato halves alternately onto the skewers. Arrange on a platter.

3 To make dipping sauce, place sour cream, mayonnaise, tomato ketchup (sauce) and Worcestershire sauce in a bowl. Stir to combine. Serve with Avocado and Prawn Skewers.

Serves 5

Curried Chicken Kebabs, Seafood Kebabs, Plugged Potatoes (page 58)

MUSHROOM AND VEGETABLE SKEWERS

4 small red onions, halved
1 fennel bulb, quartered
1 green pepper, quartered and seeded
1 red pepper, quartered and seeded
4 open mushrooms, trimmed

LEMON MARINADE
2 tablespoons sunflower oil
2 tablespoons lemon juice
2 tablespoons finely chopped fresh parsley

1 Bring a large saucepan of water to the boil. Add onion halves. Blanch for 2-3 minutes, then transfer to a colander with a slotted spoon. Refresh under cold running water, then drain. Repeat this process with fennel, then with peppers.

2 Cut each fennel quarter into four pieces; cut peppers into squares. Cut mushrooms into halves.

3 Thread eight wooden skewers, adding an onion half, two pieces of fennel, two red pepper squares, two green pepper squares and a mushroom half to each. Place kebabs in a shallow glass or ceramic dish.

4 To make marinade, place oil, lemon juice and parsley in a small bowl and mix to combine. Pour marinade over kebabs, cover and set aside for 1 hour.

5 Drain kebabs, reserving the marinade. Cook on a lightly oiled grill over moderate heat for 3-4 minutes or until vegetables are lightly grilled, turning frequently and brushing lightly with reserved marinade.

Serves 4

SKEWERED BEEF STRIPS

750 g/1½ lb blade or chuck steaks, each 3 cm/1½ in thick

RED WINE MARINADE
1 cup/250 mL/8 fl oz red wine
⅓ cup/90 mL/3 fl oz light olive oil
2 bay leaves, crushed
2 teaspoons prepared hot mustard
½ teaspoon dried thyme
½ teaspoon dried oregano
freshly ground black pepper

1 Cut each steak diagonally across in thin strips. Place in a single layer in a shallow dish.

2 To make marinade, place wine, oil, crushed bay leaves, mustard, thyme, oregano and pepper in a bowl. Mix well. Pour over steak strips and toss to coat. Cover and marinate in the refrigerator for 8 hours or overnight.

3 Soak 10 wooden skewers in water for 30 minutes.

4 Drain beef strips, reserving marinade. Weave beef strips onto wooden skewers.

Chicken and Leek Skewers, Mushroom and Vegetable Skewers, Skewered Beef Strips, Avocado and Prawn Skewers (page 35), Honey and Lamb Skewers, Bacon and Chilli Scallop Skewers

5 Cook on a lightly oiled barbecue grill over hot coals for 3-4 minutes or until cooked, turning frequently and brushing with reserved marinade. Serve at once, with Spicy Tomato Sauce (page 62), if liked.

Serves 5

1 To make marinade, place garlic, ginger, soy sauce, sherry and sugar in a small saucepan. Bring to the boil, stirring, then set aside to cool completely.

2 Place chicken cubes in a single layer in a shallow dish. Tuck leeks among them. Pour marinade over, cover and set aside to marinate for at least 30 minutes. Meanwhile soak 10 wooden skewers in cold water.

3 Drain chicken cubes and leeks, reserving marinade. Thread alternately onto drained skewers. Cook on a lightly oiled barbecue grill over hot coals for 4-5 minutes or until chicken is cooked, turning frequently and brushing with reserved marinade.

Serves 5

HONEY AND LAMB SKEWERS

750 g/1½ lb lamb fillets, cut into cubes
1 large eggplant (aubergine), cut into cubes
salt

HONEY MARINADE
½ cup/125 mL/4 fl oz olive oil
¼ cup/60 mL/2 fl oz dry sherry
1 clove garlic, crushed
2 tablespoons clear honey
1 tablespoon grated fresh root ginger
2 tablespoons soy sauce

1 To make marinade, place oil, sherry, garlic, honey, ginger and soy sauce in a shallow dish large enough to hold all the lamb cubes in a single layer. Mix well.

2 Add lamb cubes to marinade and toss to coat. Cover and marinate for at least 2 hours.

3 Place eggplant (aubergine) cubes in a colander, sprinkle with salt and set over a bowl for 30 minutes to drain. Meanwhile soak 10 wooden skewers in cold water.

4 Rinse eggplant cubes under cold running water, drain and pat dry with absorbent kitchen paper. Drain lamb, reserving marinade.

5 Thread eggplant and lamb cubes alternately onto skewers.

6 Cook kebabs on a lightly oiled barbecue grill over hot coals for 5-6 minutes or until lamb is cooked to your liking, turning frequently and brushing with marinade. Serve at once.

Serves 5

BACON AND CHILLI SCALLOP SKEWERS

1 kg/2 lb scallops, cleaned, or 500 g/1 lb white fish fillets, cut into 2.5 cm/1 in pieces
10 thin rashers lean rindless bacon

CHILLI MARINADE
1 tablespoon vegetable oil
2 tablespoons lemon juice
2 teaspoons paprika
½ teaspoon curry powder
pinch chilli powder
2 tablespoons sugar
½ teaspoon ground cumin
1 tablespoon finely chopped fresh coriander

1 To make marinade, place oil, lemon juice, paprika, curry powder, chilli powder, sugar, cumin and fresh coriander in a shallow dish large enough to hold all the seafood in a single layer. Mix well, add the scallops or fish pieces and toss to coat. Cover and set aside to marinate for 30 minutes.

2 Cut bacon into 7.5 cm/3 in strips. Place in a frying pan over low heat until the fat runs, then raise the heat slightly and cook for 2-3 minutes. The bacon should start to cook, but should still be soft. Using a slotted spoon, transfer to absorbent kitchen paper to drain. Soak 10 wooden skewers in cold water for 30 minutes.

3 Drain scallops or fish pieces, reserving marinade. Wrap each piece of seafood in a strip of bacon. Divide equally between the skewers.

4 Cook the skewers on a lightly oiled barbecue grill over moderately hot coals for 3-4 minutes or until the bacon is crisp and the seafood cooked.

5 Serve at once, with lemon slices, if liked.

Serves 5

CHICKEN AND LEEK SKEWERS

3 skinless chicken breast fillets, cubed
4 small leeks, cut into 2.5 cm/1 in lengths

GINGER MARINADE
1 clove garlic, crushed
2 teaspoons grated fresh root ginger
½ cup/125 mL/4 fl oz soy sauce
½ cup/125 mL/4 fl oz dry sherry
2 teaspoons sugar

MIXED SATAYS

250 g/8 oz skinless chicken breast
  fillets, sliced lengthwise into thin
  strips
250 g/8 oz beef fillet, sliced
  lengthwise into thin strips
250 g/8 oz pork fillet, sliced
  lengthwise into thin strips

MARINADE
¼ cup/60 mL/2 fl oz soy sauce
2 tablespoons fresh lime or
  lemon juice
2 cloves garlic, crushed
2 teaspoons finely grated fresh
  root ginger
1 chilli, seeded and finely chopped
1 tablespoon finely chopped fresh
  coriander

PEANUT SAUCE
½ cup/125 g/4 oz crunchy peanut
  butter
1 onion, finely chopped
2 tablespoons hoisin sauce
2 cloves garlic, crushed
½ cup/125 mL/4 fl oz coconut milk
  (see Cook's Tip, page 14)
2 tablespoons finely chopped
  fresh coriander

1   Soak 12 wooden skewers in water
for 30 minutes. To make sauce, place
peanut butter, onion, hoisin sauce,
garlic and coconut milk in a blender
or food processor; process until
smooth. Scrape into a bowl, stir in
coriander and set aside.

2   Drain skewers. Weave chicken,
beef and pork strips onto skewers
and place in a shallow glass or
ceramic dish.

3   To make marinade, place soy
sauce, lime or lemon juice, garlic,
ginger, chilli and coriander in a small
bowl; mix to combine. Pour over
skewers in dish, cover and marinate
for at least 1 hour.

4   Drain kebabs, discarding
marinade. Cook on a lightly oiled
barbecue grill over hot coals for 5-6
minutes or until meats are cooked.
Serve at once, with the smooth
peanut sauce.

Serves 6

VEGETABLE KEBABS WITH MUSTARD SAUCE
Illustrated on page 15

3 zucchini (courgettes), cut into
  chunks
1 eggplant (aubergine), cut into
  chunks
12 small onions, peeled
12 firm cherry tomatoes
12 button mushrooms, trimmed

MUSTARD SAUCE
15 g/½ oz butter
6 spring onions, finely chopped
2 tablespoons wholegrain mustard
1¼ cups/300 ml/10 fl oz sour cream
½ teaspoon ground cumin

1   Bring a saucepan of water to the
boil and blanch zucchini (courgettes),
aubergine and onions for 2-3
minutes. Drain vegetables in a
colander, refresh under cold running
water and drain again.

2   Start making sauce by melting
butter in a small saucepan and
cooking spring onions for 1-2 minutes
until soft. Keep warm at edge of
barbecue grill, but do not allow to
cook further.

3   Thread zucchini chunks, eggplant
chunks, onions, tomatoes and
mushrooms alternately onto 12 lightly
oiled metal skewers.

4   Cook on a lightly oiled barbecue
grill over moderately hot coals for 5
minutes or until vegetables are
golden and tender, turning frequently.

5   Stir mustard, sour cream and
cumin into sauce. Cook over low heat
for 1 minute or until sauce is heated
through. Do not allow sauce to boil or
it will curdle.

6   Transfer kebabs to individual
plates, spoon sauce over and serve
at once.

Serves 6

*Oriental Rice Salad and Pickled
Vegetable Salad (both on page 24),
Mixed Satays*

MEAT – THE MAIN ATTRACTION

Barbecue cooks are an adventurous breed, eager to try new flavourings and constantly experimenting with special sauces. Yet they can be surprisingly predictable when it comes to choosing what to cook, with burgers, sausages and chicken drumsticks top of the list. This chapter takes a fresh look at meat and poultry.

◆ ◆ ◆

BARBECUED BEEF ON BEARNAISE BREAD

750 g/1½ lb beef fillet in the piece, trimmed
1 tablespoon chopped fresh tarragon or 1 teaspoon dried tarragon
2 tablespoons sunflower oil
3 tablespoons white wine
watercress, to garnish
finely chopped fresh parsley, to serve

BEARNAISE BREAD
3 tablespoons white wine vinegar
3 tablespoons white wine
3 spring onions, finely chopped
1 tablespoon chopped fresh tarragon or 1 teaspoon dried
125 g/4 oz butter, diced, at room temperature
freshly ground black pepper
1 French bread stick

1 Tie meat at regular intervals with kitchen string, so that it retains its shape during cooking. Place it in a shallow glass or ceramic dish. Combine tarragon, oil and wine in a jug, mix well and pour over meat in dish. Cover and marinate overnight in the refrigerator.

2 Make the Béarnaise Bread. Combine vinegar, wine, spring onions and tarragon in a small saucepan.

3 Bring to the boil, then lower the heat and simmer until liquid is reduced to about 2 tablespoons. Remove from heat and set aside to cool completely.

4 Place diced butter in a blender or food processor. Add vinegar mixture with black pepper to taste. Process until mixture is smooth, then scrape into a bowl.

5 Slice bread stick, spread each slice with the flavoured butter and reassemble the loaf. Wrap in foil and refrigerate until required.

6 Drain beef, discarding marinade. Sear on all sides on a lightly oiled barbecue grill, then move to a cooler section of the grill and cook, turning frequently, for 15-20 minutes or until cooked to your liking. Place beef on side of barbecue to keep warm.

7 Add foil-wrapped bread to barbecue grill and heat through. Separate slices and arrange on a large platter. Slice meat thinly and place 1 slice on each bread round. Garnish with watercress. Offer plenty of chopped fresh parsley and black pepper as accompaniments.

Serves 10

Barbecued Beef on Béarnaise Bread

GREEK KEBABS
Illustrated on page 77

**1 kg/2 lb lean leg lamb, cut into
  2 cm/¾ in cubes**
8 small onions, peeled
**2 tomatoes, quartered, or 8 cherry
  tomatoes**
**2 zucchini (courgettes), thickly
  sliced**
8 button mushrooms
24 bay leaves
salt
olive oil for brushing

MARINADE
½ cup/125 mL/4 fl oz olive oil
⅓ cup/90 mL/3 fl oz dry white wine
2 cloves garlic, crushed
½ mild onion, finely chopped
**1 teaspoon finely chopped fresh
  mint**
1 teaspoon dried oregano
2 bay leaves
freshly ground black pepper

1 To make marinade, combine oil
and wine in a shallow dish large
enough to hold all the lamb cubes in
a single layer. Add garlic, onion, mint,
oregano and bay leaves, with black
pepper to taste.

2 Add lamb cubes to marinade,
turning to coat them thoroughly in the
mixture. Cover the dish and marinate
in the refrigerator for 12-24 hours,
turning the meat occasionally.

3 Bring a small saucepan of water
to the boil, add onions and cook until
just tender. Drain and set aside.

4 Drain lamb cubes, reserving
marinade. Thread onto eight lightly
oiled metal skewers, alternating with
the poached onions, tomato quarters
or cherry tomatoes, zucchini
(courgette) slices, mushrooms and
bay leaves. Brush kebabs with the
reserved marinade and season with
salt.

5 Cook kebabs on an oiled
barbecue grill over hot coals for
10-15 minutes. Baste frequently but
sparingly with the reserved marinade,
taking care as the oil will cause the
fire to flare.

Serves 4

---

*Falafels (page 32) with Minted Yogurt
(page 62), Honey and Sage Pork Chops*

HONEY AND SAGE PORK CHOPS

6 pork chops

HONEY SAGE MARINADE
½ cup/170 g/5½ oz clear honey
1 cup/250 mL/8 fl oz dry white wine
**1 tablespoon finely chopped fresh
  sage or 1 teaspoon dried sage**

1 To make marinade, place honey
in a small bowl. Stir in a little of the
wine, then gradually add the rest,
stirring until the mixture is smooth.
Add the sage.

2 Place chops in a single layer in a
shallow glass or creamic dish. Pour
marinade over and turn chops until
well coated.

3 Cover dish. Marinate chops for
2-3 hours at room temperature, or
overnight in the refrigerator.

4 Drain chops, discarding marinade.
Cook on an oiled barbecue grill over
hot coals for 5-6 minutes on each
side, or until cooked to your liking.
Serve at once, with a simple salad
garnish.

Serves 6

Cook's Tips: Try this recipe with
lamb chops for a delicious change.
Buy double loin chops if possible.
Thick and meaty, they are ideal for
cooking on the barbecue. Substitute
red wine vinegar for half the wine in
the marinade and add 2 teaspoons
soy sauce. Reduce the marinating
time to 2 hours, turning the chops
over halfway through. Serve with
Minted Yogurt (page 62).

ORIENTAL PORK FILLETS

1 kg/2 lb pork fillets
1 cucumber, sliced into thin
wedges
1 large tomato, sliced
cress

ORIENTAL MARINADE
⅓ cup/90 mL/3 fl oz hoisin sauce
⅓ cup/90 mL/3 fl oz tomato sauce
(ketchup)
2 tablespoons soy sauce
4 tablespoons clear honey
2 cloves garlic, crushed
2 teaspoons grated fresh root
ginger
1 teaspoon sweet chilli sauce
1 teaspoon five spice powder

1 Make marinade by mixing hoisin sauce, tomato sauce (ketchup), soy sauce, honey and garlic in a small bowl. Stir in ginger, chilli sauce and five spice powder until thoroughly combined.

2 Place pork fillets in a single layer in a shallow glass or ceramic dish, pour marinade over and turn the fillets until well coated. Cover the dish and refrigerate for 8 hours or overnight, turning the fillets once or twice.

3 Drain pork fillets, reserving the marinade in a small bowl. Place fillets on a lightly oiled barbecue grill over hot coals, turning until seared on all sides.

Barbecued Potato Skins (page 58)
Oriental Pork Fillets

4 Move fillets to a cooler part of the barbecue grill. Cook for about 15 minutes more, turning several times and brushing the fillets frequently with the reserved marinade. When the fillets are cooked through, cut them into slices and serve on individual plates. Garnish each portion with 3 cucumber wedges, a slice of tomato and a sprinkling of cress.

Serves 8

43

CHILLI PORK SPARERIBS

6 small pork back rib racks
freshly ground black pepper
½ cup/125 mL/4 fl oz apple juice
¼ cup/60 mL/2 fl oz freshly
** squeezed lime juice**
dash Tabasco sauce

APPLE CHILLI GLAZE
1 tablespoon sunflower oil
2 onions, finely chopped
2 cloves garlic, crushed
1 red chilli, seeded and finely
** chopped**
½ cup/125 g/4 oz canned apple
** purée**
1 cup/315 g/10 oz apple or
** redcurrant jelly**
½ cup/125 mL/4 fl oz apple juice
2 tablespoons fresh lime juice

1 Season ribs with black pepper and place in a single layer in a shallow glass or ceramic dish. Combine apple juice, lime juice and Tabasco in a jug or bowl, pour over ribs and toss to coat. Cover and refrigerate for 1-2 hours.

2 Make glaze. Heat oil in a saucepan and cook onions, garlic and chopped chilli over moderate heat for 10 minutes or until onions are soft. Stir in apple purée, apple or redcurrant jelly and apple juice. Bring to simmering point and simmer, stirring frequently, for 15 minutes or until mixture thickens. Stir in lime juice, with black pepper to taste. Simmer for 15 minutes more. Keep warm at side of barbecue.

3 Drain ribs, discarding marinade. Cook on a lightly oiled barbecue grill over hot coals for 5 minutes each side or until cooked through, brushing frequently with the warm glaze.

4 Serve 1 rack per person, with saffron rice, if liked.

Serves 6

Cook's Tip: Apple Chilli Glaze is equally delicious when brushed over pork chops or gammon slices.

WARM THAI BEEF SALAD

1 kg/2 lb rump steak, cut into
** 2.5 cm/1 in thick steaks**
1 cucumber, peeled and thinly
** sliced**

CORIANDER MARINADE
4 tablespoons soy sauce
2 tablespoons sunflower oil
1 teaspoon ground coriander
1 tablespoon finely chopped fresh
** coriander**
1 tablespoon soft light brown
** sugar**
freshly ground black pepper

GARNISH
fresh coriander leaves
1 red chilli, seeded and sliced

1 Make marinade by mixing soy sauce, oil, ground coriander and fresh coriander in a shallow glass or ceramic dish large enough to hold all the steaks in a single layer. Stir in sugar and add black pepper to taste.

2 Add steaks to dish, turning to coat on all sides. Cover dish and marinate steaks for at least 1 hour.

3 Arrange cucumber slices in overlapping rows on a large platter. Cover closely and chill until required.

4 Drain steaks, reserving marinade in a small saucepan. Sear steaks on a lightly oiled barbecue grill over high heat, then move to a cooler part of the grill and cook for 3 minutes each side or until cooked to your liking.

5 Bring marinade to the boil, lower the heat and simmer for 3-4 minutes. Thinly slice steaks and arrange on top of cucumber. Spoon marinade/sauce over and garnish with coriander leaves and chilli slices. Serve at once.

Serves 8

Chilli Pork Spareribs, Margaritas
(page 9)

PORK STEAKS WITH APPLE STUFFING

6 pork butterfly steaks

APPLE STUFFING
30 g/1 oz butter
1 onion, finely chopped
2 rashers rindless streaky bacon, chopped
1 apple, peeled, cored and finely chopped
1½ cups/90 g/3 oz fresh white breadcrumbs
1 egg, lightly beaten
155 g/5 oz mozzarella cheese, cubed
2 tablespoons chopped fresh parsley
freshly ground black pepper

1   Place pork steaks on a board and flatten slightly with a meat mallet or rolling pin.

2   Make stuffing. Melt butter in a frying pan and cook onion and bacon for 4-5 minutes or until bacon is crisp. Add apple and cook for 2-3 minutes until soft. Tip mixture into a bowl and stir in breadcrumbs, egg, mozzarella and parsley, with freshly ground black pepper to taste. Mix well.

3   Place a little of the stuffing on each pork steak, fold over and secure with toothpicks (cocktail sticks). Cook on a lightly oiled barbecue grill over moderately high heat for 5-6 minutes each side or until steaks are cooked. Serve at once.

Serves 6

MARINATED LEG OF LAMB

1.5-2 kg/3-4 lb leg of lamb, butterflied (see Cook's Tip)
freshly ground black pepper

LEMON HERB MARINADE
2 cloves garlic, crushed
¼ cup/60 mL/2 fl oz olive oil
¼ cup/60 mL/2 fl oz lemon juice
1 tablespoon finely chopped fresh marjoram or 1 teaspoon dried marjoram
1 tablespoon finely chopped fresh thyme or 1 teaspoon dried thyme

1   Lay lamb out flat and season well with black pepper.

2   Mix all the marinade ingredients in a large shallow glass or ceramic dish. Add the lamb, turning to coat it well. Cover the dish and marinate the lamb at cool room temperature for 3-4 hours or overnight in the refrigerator.

3   Remove lamb, reserving the marinade. Cook on a lightly oiled barbecue grill over hot coals, turning several times and basting frequently with the reserved marinade, for 15-25 minutes or until cooked to your liking.

Serves 6

Cook's Tip: Ask your butcher to butterfly the leg of lamb, or do it yourself: Place joint skin side down, thick end facing. Cut around the edges of the pelvic bone where it emerges at the thick end, to loosen it. Continue to cut around this bone until you have freed it at the joint with the leg bone. Remove the shank bone by holding it at the tip and cutting close to the bone until you reach the joint with the leg bone. Cut through the tendons and ease the shank bone out. Remove the leg bone tunnel-fashion by gently loosening the meat at either end and scraping away the meat until the bone can be eased out. Then place the knife horizontally in the leg bone cavity and partially split the meat open. Turn the flap out and spread the meat flat. Make a similar cut in the thick muscle opposite and open it out flat, too.

LAMB CUTLETS WITH HONEY BUTTER

1 tablespoon sunflower oil
1 clove garlic, crushed
8 lamb cutlets

HONEY BUTTER
90 g/3 oz butter, softened
2 tablespoons chopped fresh mint
1 tablespoon clear honey
freshly ground black pepper

1 Make the honey butter. Cream the butter with the mint and honey in a small bowl. Add black pepper to taste and mix well. Place mixture on plastic food wrap and roll to a cylindrical shape. Tuck in ends of food wrap neatly and refrigerate until firm.

2 Mix oil and garlic in a small bowl. Wrap ends of cutlet bones in foil to prevent them from burning during cooking. Brush cutlets generously with oil and garlic mixture.

3 Cook cutlets on an oiled barbecue plate (griddle) over hot coals for 3 minutes each side or until tender. Remove foil shields from cutlets, place a slice of honey butter on each and serve at once.

Serves 4

Lamb Cutlets with Honey Butter, Grilled Corn Bread (page 66)

CHILLI HONEY DRUMSTICKS

10 chicken drumsticks

CHILLI HONEY MARINADE
½ cup/170 g/5½ oz clear honey
½ cup/125 mL/4 fl oz lemon juice
1 clove garlic, crushed
pinch chilli powder

1   Make marinade. Place honey in a bowl and gradually stir in lemon juice. Add garlic and chilli powder; mix well.

2   Arrange drumsticks in a single layer in a shallow glass or ceramic dish. Pour marinade over and turn to coat thoroughly. Cover dish and marinate drumsticks for at least 2 hours at cool room temperature, or overnight in the refrigerator.

3   Drain drumsticks, reserving marinade in a bowl or jug. Cook on a lightly oiled barbecue grill over moderately hot coals for 15 minutes each side or until tender, brushing frequently with the reserved marinade and turning occasionally.

Serves 5-10

FOIL-WRAPPED CHICKEN BREASTS

60 g/2 oz butter
1 small onion, chopped
1 clove garlic, crushed
2 cups/125 g/4 oz fresh white breadcrumbs
3 tablespoons finely chopped fresh parsley
freshly ground black pepper
6 skinless chicken breast fillets
oil for brushing

1   Melt 15 g/½ oz of the butter in a small frying pan. Add onion and garlic and cook over moderate heat for 3-4 minutes or until softened.

2   Place breadcrumbs in a bowl and add onion mixture and parsley. Melt remaining butter in pan and stir into crumb mixture. Add pepper to taste.

3   Place chicken breasts between sheets of greaseproof paper and flatten slightly with a meat mallet or rolling pin. Cut six squares of foil, each large enough to enclose one chicken breast comfortably. Brush foil lightly with oil and place a chicken fillet on each square.

4   Top one half of each fillet with a little of the stuffing, then fold the rest of the fillet over the top. Bring up sides of foil to enclose chicken, sealing well.

5   Bake foil parcels on a barbecue grill over hot coals for about 20 minutes or until chicken is cooked through, turning halfway through cooking. Transfer foil parcels to individual plates and turn foil back to serve.

Serves 6

CHICKEN WITH CREAMY PESTO STUFFING

2 x 1.5 kg/3 lb chickens

CREAMY PESTO STUFFING
45 g/1½ oz basil leaves, or a mixture of basil and parsley
60 g/2 oz pine nuts
60 g/2 oz Parmesan cheese, finely grated
220 g/7 oz full fat soft cheese

1   Make the stuffing. Combine basil leaves (or basil and parsley leaves), pine nuts and Parmesan in a blender or food processor; process until finely chopped. Add full fat soft cheese and process until thoroughly combined. Scrape into a bowl.

2   Using a cleaver or sharp kitchen shears, cut each chicken in half through the backbone. Lay the half chickens on a board, skin side down, and carefully cut away the ribs and backbone, using a small sharp knife. Turn the chicken halves over and press to flatten.

3   Using clean fingers or the handle of a wooden spoon, loosen skin over breast, thigh and leg of each chicken half. Do not attempt to loosen skin on wings. Push stuffing under loosened skin, then thread a metal skewer through wing and leg of each chicken half to hold it securely.

4   Cook the stuffed chicken halves on a lightly oiled barbecue plate (griddle) over moderately hot coals for 15-20 minutes each side or until thoroughly cooked. Separate thighs from wing/breast joints to serve.

Serves 6-8

Brown Ale Damper (page 64), Chicken with Creamy Pesto Stuffing, Blue Cheese Caesar Salad (page 22)

CARIBBEAN SPATCHCOCKS

3 spatchcocks (poussins), halved
2 tablespoons crushed black peppercorns
1 teaspoon ground coriander
1 lime, cut into wedges, to garnish

LIME MARINADE
3 tablespoons white rum
2 teaspoons finely grated lime rind
1 tablespoon fresh lime juice
2 tablespoons honey
2 cloves garlic, crushed
1 teaspoon grated fresh root ginger

1 Make marinade. Place rum, lime rind and juice, honey, garlic and ginger in a bowl. Mix well.

2 Arrange spatchcock (poussin) halves in a shallow glass or ceramic dish. Add the marinade, spooning it all over the birds. Cover the dish and marinate for 1 hour.

3 Thread a skewer through the wings and legs of each spatchcock half; brush with any remaining marinade. Combine crushed peppercorns and coriander in a small bowl; press onto skin of birds.

4 Cook on a lightly oiled barbecue grill over moderately hot coals for 20-30 minutes or until cooked, turning frequently.

Serves 6

ALMOND ORANGE DRUMSTICKS

8 chicken drumsticks
90 g/3 oz butter, softened
1 tablespoon finely grated orange rind
4 tablespoons ground almonds
1 tablespoon finely chopped fresh parsley

1 Bring a large saucepan of water to the boil. Add chicken drumsticks and allow water to return to boiling point. Lower heat and simmer for 10 minutes, then drain chicken; cool slightly.

2 Cream butter in a small bowl. Stir in grated orange rind, almonds and parsley, mixing well.

3 Gently ease the skin away from the flesh on each drumstick. Spread the almond mixture over the flesh, taking care not to break the skin.

4 Cook on a lightly oiled barbecue grill over hot coals for 10-15 minutes, turning frequently, until drumsticks are golden and cooked through.

Serves 4

Cook's Tips: Chicken must always be served well cooked, and it is therefore a good idea to parcook it before barbecuing, as in this recipe. If preferred, parcook the drumsticks in the microwave. Arrange them around the edge of a large circular platter, with the narrow ends pointing inwards. Cook for 10 minutes on Full Power, turning drumsticks once. Cool slightly, then spread the flesh with the almond mixture and transfer the drumsticks to the barbecue to finish cooking.

Softened cream cheese may be used instead of butter. Ground hazelnuts may be substituted for the ground almonds.

Caribbean Spatchcocks

SPICY CHICKEN FAJITAS

6 skinless chicken breast fillets
2 onions, thinly sliced
2 tablespoons sunflower oil
6 flour tortillas or tacos
accompaniments, see Cook's Tip

LIME MARINADE
½ cup/125 mL/4 fl oz fresh lime
juice
½ cup/125 mL/4 fl oz sunflower oil
1 red chilli, seeded and finely
chopped

1 To make marinade, combine lime juice, oil and chilli in a shallow glass or ceramic dish which is large enough to hold all the chicken breasts in a single layer.

2 Add chicken and onions, turning to coat in the marinade. Cover and marinate for 2-3 hours, turning chicken breasts occasionally.

3 Drain chicken and onions, discarding marinade. Heat oil in a frying pan on the barbecue grill and cook onions for 10-15 minutes or until golden. Cook chicken on the lightly oiled barbecue grill for 5-7 minutes or until cooked through, turning frequently. Warm tortillas or tacos on the edge of the barbecue.

4 Slice the cooked chicken into strips and arrange on a large platter with the onions. Add the tortillas or tacos. Serve at once, with the accompaniments in separate bowls.

Spicy Corn Cobs (page 57), Warm Bean and Vegetable Salad (page 18) and Spicy Chicken Fajitas

Guests help themselves to tortillas or tacos and add the fillings or toppings of their choice.

Serves 6

Cook's Tip: The accompaniments traditionally served with Spicy Chicken Fajitas are diced avocado (tossed with lemon juice to prevent discoloration), diced peeled tomatoes, finely chopped spring onions and grated tasty cheese (mature Cheddar). Add a bowl each of natural yogurt and finely chopped fresh coriander.

CAJUN CHICKEN WINGS

12 chicken wings
3 bay leaves
3 cloves garlic, chopped
½ teaspoon caraway seeds
½ teaspoon ground mace
½ teaspoon cayenne pepper
1 teaspoon paprika
½ teaspoon ground coriander
½ teaspoon ground cumin
1 teaspoon mustard powder
3 tablespoons tomato paste (purée)
3 tablespoons lemon juice

1   Remove any feathers remaining on chicken wings; cut off wing tips. Bring a large saucepan of water to the boil. Add chicken wings and allow water to return to boiling point. Lower heat and simmer for 10 minutes, then drain chicken; cool slightly.

2   Crumble bay leaves into a mortar (see Cook's Tip). Using a pestle, grind finely, then add garlic cloves and caraway seeds; grind well. Add mace, cayenne, paprika, coriander, cumin and mustard; grind until well mixed. Beat in tomato paste (purée) and lemon juice.

3   Brush one side of each chicken wing generously with spice mixture. Place the wings, spice side up, on a lightly oiled barbecue grill over moderately hot coals. Cook for 10 minutes, then turn over and brush the other side with spice mixture. Grill for 10 minutes more, until wings are crisp and well cooked.

Serves 4

Cook's Tip: If you do not have a mortar and pestle, improvise by using a bowl and the end of a rolling pin.

CITRUS-GLAZED TURKEY

½ cup/125 mL/4 fl oz olive oil
1 cup/250 mL/8 fl oz fresh orange juice
2 tablespoons lemon juice
1 tablespoon grated orange rind
1 tablespoon finely chopped fresh thyme
2 tablespoons finely chopped fresh parsley
2 cloves garlic, crushed
6 turkey breast steaks, total weight about 750 g/1½ lb

SAUCE
1 cup/315 g/10 oz redcurrant jelly
1 teaspoon grated orange rind
4 tablespoons freshly squeezed orange juice
1 tablespoon Dijon mustard
¼ teaspoon soft light brown sugar

1   Combine the olive oil, orange juice, lemon juice, orange rind, thyme, parsley and garlic in a shallow glass or ceramic dish large enough to hold the turkey steaks in a single layer. Add the turkey and turn to coat in the mixture. Cover the dish and marinate the turkey for 2 hours in the refrigerator.

2   Make the sauce by mixing all the ingredients in a small saucepan. Bring to the boil, stirring, then lower the heat and simmer for 5 minutes. Keep warm on the edge of the barbecue grill.

3   Drain the turkey, reserving the marinade. Cook on a lightly oiled barbecue grill over moderately hot coals for 5 minutes each side or until cooked through. Brush frequently with the reserved marinade.

4   Serve the turkey steaks on individual plates, with the sauce.

Serves 6

TANDOORI CHICKEN DRUMSTICKS

12 plump chicken drumsticks
1 teaspoon salt
3 tablespoons lemon juice

MARINADE
4 cloves garlic, crushed
2 cups/500 g/1 lb natural yogurt
1 tablespoon white wine vinegar
½ teaspoon ground cumin
½ teaspoon ground ginger
½ teaspoon chilli powder
1 teaspoon ground coriander
1 teaspoon garam masala
1 tablespoon tomato paste (purée)

1   Skin the drumsticks. Using a sharp knife, cut several deep parallel slashes in each drumstick. Rub the salt and lemon juice into the cuts. Put the drumsticks in a shallow glass or ceramic dish, cover and set aside for 30 minutes.

2   Make the marinade by mixing the crushed garlic with the yogurt and vinegar in a bowl. Stir in the cumin, ginger, chilli powder, coriander, garam masala and tomato paste (purée). Mix well.

3   Drain the drumsticks, discarding the liquid, and pat dry with absorbent kitchen paper. Return to the clean dish and pour the yogurt mixture over. Turn the drumsticks to coat them in the mixture, making sure that it penetrates the slashes. Cover the dish tightly and marinate the chicken overnight in the refrigerator.

4   Carefully transfer the drumsticks, with as much of the marinade as possible, to an oiled barbecue plate (griddle) over hot coals. Grill for about 10 minutes each side, or until cooked through. Garnish with raw onion rings and lemon wedges, and serve on a bed of lettuce, if liked.

Serves 6

VEGETABLES

Add colour and flavour to your barbecue grill with a variety of vegetables. Char-grilling turns peppers, zucchini (courgettes), tomatoes and mild red onions into a taste sensation, while more delicate vegetables are delicious when cooked in foil parcels.

◆ ◆ ◆

CHAR-GRILLED VEGETABLE SLICES

½ cup/125 mL/4 fl oz olive oil
1 clove garlic, crushed
1 large eggplant (aubergine), cut lengthwise into thick slices
3 large zucchini (courgettes), cut lengthwise into thick slices
2 red peppers, cut into quarters, seeded
3 firm beefsteak tomatoes, cut into thick slices
freshly ground black pepper

1 Whisk oil and garlic in a small bowl until combined. Brush eggplant (aubergine), zucchini (courgette), red pepper and tomato slices with the oil mixture.

2 Cook the eggplant, zucchini and pepper slices on a lightly oiled barbecue grill over moderately hot coals for 4-5 minutes or until almost cooked. Add tomato slices and cook for 2-3 minutes more. Serve with Skewered Potatoes and Onions (right) and pork sausages or a vegetarian equivalent.

Serves 6

SKEWERED POTATOES AND ONIONS

12 baby new potatoes, scrubbed
3 red onions
olive oil for brushing

1 Boil, steam or microwave potatoes until just tender. Thread in pairs on six small oiled metal skewers.

2 Cut the red onions into quarters, leaving enough of the root end in place to keep the layers together. Thread the quarters in pairs on six small oiled metal skewers.

3 Brush the potatoes and onion quarters with olive oil and cook on a lightly oiled barbecue grill over moderately hot coals, turning halfway through cooking. The onions will require 15-20 minutes and the potatoes 10-15 minutes.

Serves 6

Cook's Tip: Flavour the olive oil with finely chopped herbs, such as basil, oregano, thyme or rosemary. Alternatively, add a drop of Tabasco sauce to the oil before brushing it over the potatoes and onions.

Char-grilled Vegetable Slices and Skewered Potatoes and Onions, served with herby sausages

MUSHROOM BROCHETTES

2 red onions
16 button mushrooms, trimmed
**½ red pepper, cored, seeded and
    cut into 8 strips**
**4 large flat mushrooms or oyster
    mushrooms, trimmed and halved**
8 bay leaves
**½ yellow pepper, cored, seeded
    and cut into 8 strips**
60 g/2 oz butter, melted
chopped fresh herbs to garnish

1 Cut the red onions into quarters, leaving enough of the root end in place to keep the layers together. Bring a saucepan of water to the boil, add the onion quarters and cook for 5 minutes. Drain well.

2 Thread one onion quarter onto each of eight metal skewers. Add 1 button mushroom, then a strip of red pepper followed by half a flat mushroom or oyster mushroom. Complete each skewer by adding 1 bay leaf, 1 strip of yellow pepper and another button mushroom.

3 Brush all the brochettes thoroughly with melted butter. Cook on a lightly oiled barbecue grill over moderately hot coals for 10 minutes, brushing frequently with the remaining melted butter. Sprinkle with the chopped herbs and serve.

Makes 8

Cook's Tip: The heat under the brochettes should not be too intense. Raise the barbecue grill if possible or cook the brochettes towards the edge.

MUSHROOM MEDLEY

30 g/1 oz butter
2 tablespoons sunflower oil
**125 g/4 oz button mushrooms,
    trimmed and thinly sliced**
**125 g/4 oz oyster mushrooms,
    trimmed and torn into pieces**
**125 g/4 oz shiitake or chestnut
    mushrooms, trimmed and thinly
    sliced**
**1 tablespoon sesame seeds,
    toasted**
salt
freshly ground black pepper
1 teaspoon sesame oil
snipped fresh chives, to garnish

1 Melt butter in oil in a frying pan. Add all the mushrooms. Fry over moderate to high heat for 2 minutes, stirring constantly but taking care not to break the mushrooms up.

2 Remove the pan from the heat, add sesame seeds and toss with mushrooms. Add salt and pepper to taste.

3 Prepare a square of foil, large enough to comfortably enclose mushroom mixture. Place the foil square shiny side up, spoon mushroom mixture into the centre and drizzle with sesame oil. Bring up the sides of the foil to make a loose but secure package.

4 Place the foil package on a barbecue grill over moderately hot coals for about 10 minutes, or until mushrooms are hot and tender, and flavours have combined. Open the foil carefully, tip the contents into a bowl, sprinkle with chives and serve.

Serves 4

Mushroom Brochettes, Mushroom Medley

FRIED ONION RINGS

1 mild onion, sliced into 5mm/¼ in rings
oil for deep frying

BATTER
1 cup/125 g/4 oz plain white flour
pinch salt
2 tablespoons olive oil
⅔ cup/170 mL/5½ fl oz tepid water
2 large egg whites

1 Make batter. Sift flour and salt into a bowl. Make a well in the centre and pour in olive oil and tepid water. Stir with a wooden spoon, gradually incorporating flour from the sides of the well, until the mixture forms a smooth batter with the consistency of thick cream. If batter is too thick, add a little more tepid water. Cover bowl and set batter aside for 30 minutes at room temperature.

2 Whisk egg whites in a clean grease-free bowl until stiff but not dry; fold into batter gently but thoroughly.

3 Heat oil for deep frying to a temperature of 190°C/375°F or until a cube of bread added to the oil browns in 50 seconds.

4 Dip several onion rings at a time into batter, then fry for 1 minute or until golden brown. Drain on absorbent kitchen paper. When all the onion rings have been cooked, reheat them if necessary by frying them again very briefly just before serving.

Serves 4

SPICY CORN COBS
Illustrated on page 51

125 g/4 oz butter, softened
1 small red chilli, seeded and finely chopped
2 tablespoons grated Parmesan cheese
1 tablespoon finely chopped fresh coriander
6 corn cobs, husks removed

1 Place butter, chopped chilli, Parmesan and coriander in a blender or food processor; process until smooth and combined, then scrape into a bowl and chill until required.

2 Wrap corn cobs in a double thickness of foil and cook on a barbecue grill over moderately hot coals for 30-35 minutes or until tender. To serve, open foil and spread corn cobs with chilli butter.

Serves 6

BARBECUE CHIPS
Illustrated on pages 28-29

500 g/1 lb potatoes, peeled and cut crosswise into 5 mm/¼ in slices
500 g/1 lb parsnips, peeled and cut crosswise into 5 mm/¼ in slices
500 g/1 lb sweet potatoes, peeled and cut crosswise into 5 mm/¼ in slices
3 tablespoons olive oil
4 onions, chopped

Fried Onion Rings

1 Bring a large saucepan of water to the boil and add sliced potatoes, parsnips and sweet potatoes. Blanch for 2 minutes.

2 Drain the vegetable slices, refresh under cold running water and drain again. Dry between sheets of absorbent kitchen paper.

3 Heat oil in a large frying pan on barbecue grill over hot coals. Add onions and cook for 15-20 minutes or until golden and crisp. Add potato, parsnip and sweet potato slices and cook for 10 minutes or until chips are tender. Serve at once.

Serves 10

BARBECUED POTATO SKINS

6 large baking potatoes, scrubbed
olive oil
salt
Creamy Cheese Dip or Tomato
   Anchovy Dip (both on page 6)
   to serve

1 Preheat oven to 200°C, 400°F, Gas 6. Bake potatoes directly on an oven shelf for 1 hour or until tender, then transfer to a rack and set aside until cool enough to handle. Cut potatoes in half, scooping out flesh to leave a 5 mm/¼ in thick shell. Reserve potato flesh for use in another recipe.

2 Cut potato skins into large pieces; brush with oil. Cook on a lightly oiled barbecue plate (griddle) over moderately hot coals for 5-8 minutes on each side or until crisp and golden. Add salt to taste and serve with the dip of your choice.

Serves 4

VEGETABLE FOIL PARCELS

2 rashers rindless streaky bacon,
   chopped (optional)
375 g/12 oz cooked brown rice
2 tablespoons chopped fresh
   parsley
3 carrots, chopped
3 courgettes (zucchini), topped,
   tailed and chopped
12 broccoli florets
30 g/1 oz butter
3 tablespoons snipped fresh
   chives
125 g/4 oz tasty cheese (mature
   Cheddar), grated

1 Prepare six squares of foil, each about 30 x 24 cm/12 x 9½ in).

2 If using bacon, heat it gently in a heavy-bottomed pan until the fat runs, then raise the heat and fry until pieces are crisp. Drain on absorbent kitchen paper.

3 Combine rice and parsley in a bowl. Add bacon, if using. Divide evenly between foil squares.

4 Boil, steam or microwave vegetables until crisp-tender. Drain well, then arrange on top of rice mixture. Dot with butter.

5 Mix chives and grated cheese in a small bowl. Divide mixture between foil squares, then close the parcels loosely but securely.

6 Cook the foil packages on a barbecue grill over moderately hot coals for about 15 minutes or until mixture is hot and vegetables are tender. Transfer packages to individual plates, open to reveal the contents and serve.

Serves 6

GARLIC AND HERB POTATO ROUNDS
Illustrated on page 13

4 potatoes, peeled and thinly
   sliced
60 g/2 oz butter, melted
1 teaspoon paprika
1 clove garlic, crushed
1 teaspoon dried mixed herbs

1 Dry potato slices between sheets of absorbent kitchen paper. Combine butter, paprika, garlic and herbs in a large bowl. Add the potato rounds and toss to coat.

2 Cook the potato rounds on a lightly oiled barbecue plate (griddle) for 8-10 minutes or until golden brown and tender. Baste occasionally with any remaining butter mixture. Serve at once.

Serves 4

PLUGGED POTATOES
Illustrated on pages 34-35

6 large baking potatoes, scrubbed
1 tablespoon olive oil
1 tablespoon finely chopped fresh
   rosemary
freshly ground black pepper
6 cloves garlic, peeled and cut
   in half

1 Using an apple corer, carefully remove a plug from each potato, taking care not to go right through the potato. Reserve the plugs.

2 Combine oil and rosemary in a small bowl. Add black pepper to taste.

3 Fill holes in each potato with two garlic halves and a little of the oil mixture.

4 Cut off two thirds of each plug and discard, then use a shortened plug to stopper the hole in each potato.

5 Wrap plugged potatoes in foil and cook on a barbecue grill over hot coals for 1 hour or until tender.

Serves 6

BAKED POTATOES WITH CHEESE

6 large baking potatoes, scrubbed
50 g/2 oz butter, softened
½ cup/125 mL/4 fl oz crème fraîche
   or thickened cream (double)
125 g/4 oz tasty cheese (Cheddar),
   grated
½ red pepper, cored, seeded and
   finely diced
salt
freshly ground black pepper
watercress sprigs to garnish

1 Preheat oven to 200°C, 400°F, Gas 6. Bake potatoes directly on an oven shelf for 1 hour or until tender.

2 Using a sharp knife, cut a thin lengthwise slice from each potato; set aside for use as a lid. Scoop out the flesh from each potato into a bowl, leaving a firm shell. Set shells aside.

3 Mash potato flesh throughly, then beat in butter and crème fraîche or cream, using a wooden spoon. Stir in cheese and diced red pepper, with plenty of salt and pepper to taste. Spoon mixture back into potato shells, piling it up in the centre.

4 Prepare six squares of foil, each large enough to comfortably enclose a filled potato. Wrap each potato in foil, closing the parcels securely but taking care to leave some space above the filling to prevent it from being compressed. Wrap potato lids in a separate foil parcel.

5 Cook the foil parcels on a barbecue grill over moderately hot coals for about 20 minutes, until the filling is hot. To serve, turn back foil and top potatoes with lids, placing them at an angle. Garnish with watercress.

Serves 6

Baked Potatoes with Cheese

SAUCES & MARINADES

Sauces spell success when it comes to making a barbecue memorable. Marinades moisten, tenderize and add flavour, while hot or cold sauces are the perfect accompaniments for grilled meat, fish and vegetables.

◆ ◆ ◆

SWEET AND SOUR SAUCE

1 tablespoon sunflower oil
1 small onion, chopped
1 red pepper, cored, seeded and
  chopped
1 tablespoon soy sauce
2 tablespoons honey
1 tablespoon tomato paste (purée)
2 tablespoons cornflour
½ cup/125 mL/4 fl oz cider vinegar
½ cup/125 mL/4 fl oz chicken stock
  or water
440 g/14 oz can pineapple pieces,
  drained

1 Heat oil in a saucepan. Add onion and red pepper and cook for 4-5 minutes or until soft.

2 Place soy sauce, honey, tomato paste (purée), cornflour and vinegar in a bowl. Mix well, then stir in stock or measured water.

3 Stir cornflour mixture into pan containing chopped onion and red pepper. Heat, stirring until the mixture boils and thickens. Stir in pineapple pieces and cook for 2-3 minutes more.

Makes 2 cups/500 mL/16 fl oz

MEXICAN CHILLI SAUCE

2 tablespoons sunflower oil
2 small red chillies, seeded and
  finely chopped
3 small green chillies, seeded and
  finely chopped
3 cloves garlic, crushed
2 onions, finely chopped
1 tablespoon finely chopped fresh
  coriander
440 g/14 oz can chopped tomatoes
1 teaspoon soft light brown sugar
½ teaspoon ground cinnamon
¼ teaspoon ground cloves
¼ teaspoon ground ginger
2 tablespoons lemon juice
3 tablespoons water

1 Heat oil in a frying pan. Add red and green chillies, garlic, onions and coriander. Cook for 2-3 minutes, then stir in tomatoes, brown sugar, cinnamon, cloves, ginger, lemon juice and measured water. Bring to the boil, then lower the heat and simmer for 15-20 minutes or until sauce reduces and thickens.

Makes 2 cups/500 mL/16 fl oz

BARBECUE SAUCE

1 tablespoon sunflower oil
1 onion, chopped
1 clove garlic, crushed
1 teaspoon mustard powder
1 tablespoon Worcestershire sauce
1 tablespoon soft light brown
  sugar
3 tablespoons tomato sauce
  (ketchup)
1 teaspoon chilli sauce
¾ cup/185 mL/6 fl oz beef stock
freshly ground black pepper

1 Heat oil in a saucepan, add onion and garlic and cook for 3-4 minutes or until soft. Stir in mustard powder, Worcestershire sauce, brown sugar, tomato sauce (ketchup), chilli sauce and stock. Bring to the boil, then lower the heat and simmer for 8-10 minutes or until sauce thickens and reduces slightly. Add black pepper to taste.

Makes 1 cup/250 mL/8 fl oz

Barbecue Sauce, Apple and Horseradish Sauce (page 62), Mexican Chilli Sauce, Sweet and Sour Sauce

APPLE AND HORSERADISH SAUCE

½ cup/125 mL/4 fl oz thickened
  cream (double)
1 Granny Smith apple, grated
3 tablespoons horseradish relish
freshly ground black pepper

1   Place cream in a bowl and whip
until soft peaks form. Fold in grated
apple and horseradish relish. Add
black pepper to taste. Cover closely
if not serving immediately.

Makes 1 cup/250 mL/8 fl oz

SPICY TOMATO SAUCE

1 tablespoon olive oil
1 onion, finely chopped
1 clove garlic, crushed
1 red chilli, seeded and finely
  chopped
1 green pepper, finely chopped
440 g/14 oz can chopped tomatoes
freshly ground black pepper

1   Heat oil in a saucepan and fry
onion, garlic, chilli and green pepper
for 5 minutes or until soft.

2   Add tomatoes, bring mixture to
the boil, then reduce heat and
simmer for 15-20 minutes, stirring
occasionally, until sauce thickens.
Add black pepper to taste.

Makes 2 cups/500 mL/16 fl oz

SUN-DRIED TOMATO SAUCE

6 sun-dried tomatoes, chopped
2 cloves garlic, crushed
1 tablespoon pine nuts
1 tablespoon lemon juice
½ cup/125 mL/4 fl oz olive oil
2 tablespoons grated Parmesan
  cheese
freshly ground black pepper

1   Place sun-dried tomatoes, garlic,
pine nuts and lemon juice in a
blender or food processor. Add
1 tablespoon of the oil; process until
smooth. With motor running,
gradually add remaining oil through
lid or feeder tube. Scrape sauce into
a bowl, stir in Parmesan and add
black pepper to taste.

Makes 1 cup/250 mL/8 fl oz

MINTED YOGURT

Illustrated on page 42

1 cup/250 g/8 oz natural yogurt
1 tablespoon snipped fresh chives
2 tablespoons finely chopped
  fresh mint
freshly ground black pepper

1   Place yogurt in a bowl. Stir in
chives and mint, with black pepper to
taste. Serve chilled.

Makes 1 cup/250 mL/8 fl oz

RED WINE MARINADE

(for red meat or game)

1½ cups/375 mL/12 fl oz red wine
½ cup/125 mL/4 fl oz olive oil
1 small onion, diced
1 bay leaf, torn into pieces
1 teaspoon black peppercorns,
  crushed
1 clove garlic, crushed
1 tablespoon finely chopped fresh
  thyme or 1 teaspoon dried thyme

1   Place wine, oil, onion, bay leaf,
peppercorns, garlic and thyme in a
small bowl; mix to combine.

2   Pour marinade over meat, toss to
coat, then cover and leave to
marinate.

Makes 2 cups/500 mL/16 fl oz

HOT CHILLI MARINADE

(for meat or poultry)

¼ cup/60 mL/2 fl oz soy sauce
¼ cup/60 mL/2 fl oz hoisin sauce
½ cup/125 mL/4 fl oz dry sherry
1 clove garlic, crushed
1 teaspoon grated fresh root
  ginger
2 spring onions, finely chopped
1 teaspoon hot chilli sauce

1   Place soy sauce, hoisin sauce,
sherry, garlic, ginger, spring onions
and chilli sauce in a small bowl; mix
to combine.

2   Pour marinade over meat or
poultry, toss to coat, then cover and
leave to marinate. Use marinade as a
basting sauce when barbecuing.

Makes 1 cup/250 mL/8 fl oz

WHITE WINE AND HERB MARINADE

(for poultry or fish)

¾ cup/185 mL/6 fl oz white wine
¼ cup/60 mL/2 fl oz olive oil
2 spring onions, finely chopped
1 tablespoon chopped fresh herbs
  or 1 teaspoon dried herbs

1   Place wine, oil, spring onions and
herbs in a small bowl; mix to
combine.

2   Pour marinade over poultry or
fish, toss to coat, then cover and
leave to marinate.

Makes 1 cup/250 mL/8 fl oz

● Place meat, poultry or fish for marinating in a single layer in a shallow glass or ceramic dish. Stainless steel may also be used, but avoid any material which might react adversely with the acid of the marinade. A stout polythene bag is ideal for large cuts of meat – remove as much air as possible after adding meat and marinade, and seal tightly.

● When adding the marinade, turn or toss the food lightly to coat it. Repeat this process several times during marinating.

● Cover food to be marinated and always observe safe and sensible kitchen practice: food may be marinated at room temperature for short periods in a cool kitchen, but food such as game, that benefits from a long slow marinating, should be placed in the refrigerator and brought to room temperature just before barbecuing.

● Fish (particularly tender white fish) and shelled seafood should not be marinated for more than 30 minutes or the fish will start to 'cook', due to the action of the acid in the marinade.

LEMON HERB MARINADE
(for meat – especially lamb – or poultry)

½ cup/125 mL/4 fl oz olive oil
¼ cup/60 mL/2 fl oz lemon juice
¼ cup/60 mL/2 fl oz white wine vinegar
1 clove garlic, crushed
1 teaspoon finely grated lemon rind
2 teaspoons finely chopped fresh parsley
2 teaspoons snipped fresh chives
1 tablespoon finely chopped fresh rosemary or 1 teaspoon dried rosemary

1 Place oil, lemon juice, vinegar, garlic, lemon rind, parsley, chives and rosemary in a small bowl; mix to combine.

2 Pour marinade over meat or poultry, toss to coat, then cover and leave to marinate.

Makes 1 cup/250 mL/8 fl oz

Cook's Tip: Use lime juice and rind and omit rosemary for a marinade suitable for fish.

TERIYAKI MARINADE
(for chicken, pork or beef)

½ cup/125 mL/4 fl oz soy sauce
¼ cup/90 g/3 oz clear honey
1 clove garlic, crushed
½ teaspoon ground ginger

1 Place soy sauce, honey, garlic and ginger in a small bowl; mix to combine.

2 Pour marinade over meat or pountry, toss to coat, then cover and leave to marinate.

Makes ¾ cup/185 mL/6 fl oz

BARBECUE BREADS

There's something about eating in the open air that invites the serving of freshly baked breads. Whether you actually bake the bread yourself, using the recipes for Damper, Focaccia or Corn Bread, or add a savoury filling to a French stick, the results are certain to go down well with guests of all ages.

◆ ◆ ◆

FOCACCIA

This is a simple recipe for Focaccia, using easy blend dried yeast which is added straight to the flour. The dough is very soft, but bakes to a delicious loaf.

8 cups/1 kg/2 lb strong plain white flour
6 sage leaves, finely chopped, or 2 teaspoons dried sage
1 teaspoon salt
2 sachets (2 tablespoons) easy blend dried yeast
2 cups/500 mL/16 fl oz tepid water
½ cup/125 mL/4 fl oz dry white wine
4 tablespoons olive oil

1   Sift flour into a large bowl. Add sage and salt. Stir in easy blend dried yeast.

2   Make a well in the centre of the flour mixture, pour in the tepid water, dry white wine and 2 tablespoons of the olive oil.

3   Mix well, gradually incorporating the flour from the sides of the well. The mixture will form a soft 'spoon' dough. Beat well, using floured hands if preferred, then sprinkle the surface of the dough lightly with flour, cover the bowl with plastic food wrap and set aside in a warm place for 2 hours or until the dough has doubled in bulk.

4   Preheat oven to 200°C, 400°F, Gas 6. Using a wooden spoon or floured hands, beat/knead dough briefly. The dough will be very soft.

5   Divide dough in half. Transfer each half to a large lightly oiled flan tin or pizza plate, forming it into a rough round. Using the lightly floured end of a wooden spoon, dimple the surface of each round. Brush with the remaining olive oil.

6   Bake for 25-30 minutes or until loaves are golden and sound hollow when rapped on the base. Remove from oven and invert on wire racks. Serve warm.

Makes 2 loaves

Cook's Tip: Focaccia comes in a wide variety of shapes, sizes and flavours. Try adding sliced stoned black olives or crumbled grilled bacon to the basic dough.

BROWN ALE DAMPER
Illustrated on pages 48-49

2 cups/250 g/8 oz self-raising white flour
2 cups/315 g/10 oz wholemeal flour
2 teaspoons baking powder
1 teaspoon salt
45 g/1½ oz butter, cubed
2 cups/500 mL/16 fl oz brown ale

1   Sift flours, baking powder and salt into a large mixing bowl. Return husks from sieve to bowl. Rub in butter until mixture resembles coarse breadcrumbs. Make a well in the centre of the flour mixture and pour in brown ale. Mix to a soft dough.

2   Knead dough on a lightly floured surface until smooth. Shape into a 20 cm/8 in round; score into wedges, using a sharp knife. Prepare a double square of foil large enough to enclose damper comfortably. Lightly dust foil, place damper in centre and wrap loosely but securely in foil.

3   Place foil parcel on barbecue grill over moderately hot coals for 1 hour or until cooked through, turning several times. Serve damper warm.

Makes 1 loaf

Focaccia

GRILLED CORN BREAD

Illustrated on page 47

1 cup/170 g/5½ oz corn meal
   (polenta)
¾ cup/90 g/3 oz self-raising white
   flour
½ teaspoon sugar
30 g/1 oz butter, melted
1 cup/250 mL/8 fl oz milk
1 egg
olive oil

CORIANDER PESTO
3 large bunches fresh coriander,
   leaves stripped from stems
2 cloves garlic, crushed
60 g/2 oz pine nuts
½ cup/125 mL/4 fl oz olive oil
60 g/2 oz Parmesan cheese, grated

1   Preheat oven to 180°C,350°F,
Gas 4. Grease a 20 cm/8 in round
cake tin. Place corn meal (polenta),
flour and sugar in a mixing bowl. In a
separate bowl, whisk melted butter
with milk and egg. Add to dry
ingredients and mix to a batter.

2   Spoon batter into prepared tin.
Bake for 15-20 minutes or until a
skewer inserted in the centre of the
bread comes out clean. Allow to
stand in the tin for 5 minutes, then
turn out on a wire rack to cool.

3   Make pesto by finely chopping
coriander leaves with garlic and pine
nuts in a blender or food processor.
With motor running, slowly pour in oil
through hole in lid or feeder tube until
mixture forms a thick, smooth sauce.
Add Parmesan and process to
combine.

4   Cut bread into six wedges, brush
lightly with oil, and cook on a
barbecue grill over hot coals until
golden. Transfer each wedge to a
plate, top with a spoonful of the
coriander pesto and serve at once.

Serves 6

Cook's Tip: Grilled Corn Bread also
tastes good with a richly-flavoured
tomato sauce, such as Spicy Tomato
Sauce or Sun-dried Tomato Sauce
(both on page 62).

BRUSCHETTA WITH TOMATO AND OLIVES

Illustrated on page 13

¼ cup/60 mL/2 fl oz olive oil
2 cloves garlic, crushed
8 thick slices crusty bread

TOMATO OLIVE TOPPING
3 large ripe tomatoes, peeled and
   diced
2 tablespoons finely chopped red
   pepper
6 pitted black olives, finely
   chopped
½ red onion, finely chopped
2 tablespoons finely chopped
   fresh basil
1 tablespoon olive oil
1 tablespoon balsamic or red wine
   vinegar
salt
freshly ground black pepper

1   To make topping, place tomatoes,
red pepper, olives, onion, basil, oil
and vinegar in a bowl. Add salt and
pepper to taste and toss to combine.

2   Combine oil and garlic in a small
bowl. Brush both sides of each slice
of bread with the mixture. Cook bread
on a lightly oiled barbecue grill over
moderately hot coals for 2-3 minutes
each side or until toasted. Serve
immediately, topping each slice with
a little of the tomato and olive
mixture.

Serves 4

GARLIC BREAD

1 large French stick

GARLIC BUTTER
125 g/4 oz butter, softened
2 cloves garlic, crushed
2 tablespoons finely chopped
   fresh parsley
freshly ground black pepper

1   Slice bread on a slight diagonal.
Make the cuts at 2 cm/¾ in intervals
but do not slice right through the
stick; keep slices joined at the base.

2   Make garlic butter by processing
all the ingredients in a blender or
food processor. Alternatively, cream
butter in a bowl and stir in remaining
ingredients.

3   Spread one side of each slice of
bread with garlic butter. Press slices
together to reform bread stick. Wrap
stick in foil. Heat on a barbecue grill
over moderately hot coals for 15-20
minutes or until bread is hot.

Serves 8

Cook's Tip: The easiest way to slice
the French stick without making the
mistake of cutting right through is to
place a slim board behind the stick
when slicing. Stop cutting as soon as
the knife encounters the board.

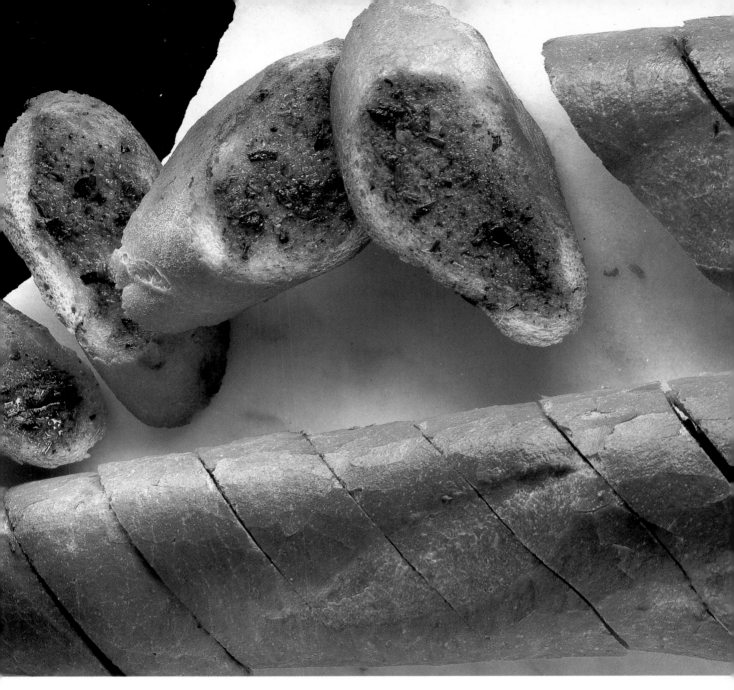

ANCHOVY AND OLIVE BREAD

1 large French stick

ANCHOVY AND OLIVE BUTTER
**½ x 60 g/2 oz can anchovy fillets,
drained and chopped
30 g/1 oz pitted black olives,
chopped
125 g/4 oz butter, softened
freshly ground black pepper
2 tablespoons snipped fresh
chives**

1   Slice bread on a slight diagonal.
Make the cuts at 2 cm/¾ in intervals
but do not slice right through the stick;
keep the slices joined at the base.

2   Make anchovy and olive butter by
pounding anchovy fillets and olives
together to a paste, then beating this
into the softened butter. Add pepper
to taste and beat in the chives.

3   Spread one side of each slice of
bread with anchovy and olive butter.
Press slices together to reform the
bread stick. Wrap stick in foil. Heat
on a barbecue grill over moderately
hot coals for 15-20 minutes or until
bread is hot.

Serves 8

Anchovy and Olive Bread

SWEET SURPRISES

The party isn't over when the fire dies down. The embers provide the perfect heat for cooking treats like Marshmallow Surprises, Fruit Kebabs and Flaming Bananas. Guests who have never sampled barbecued desserts will enjoy the novelty, especially when they are invited to help with the preparation. Alternatively, provide a cool contrast by way of ice creams, sorbets or fruit salads.

◆ ◆ ◆

MANGO ICE CREAM

8 egg yolks
1¼ cups/315 g/10 oz caster sugar
4 cups/1 litre/1¾ pt milk
2 cups/500 mL/16 fl oz thickened cream (double)
vanilla essence
250 g/8 oz fresh or drained canned mango, puréed

1 Place egg yolks and sugar in a mixing bowl. Beat until creamy.

2 Combine milk and cream in a large saucepan. Bring to the boil, then immediately remove from the heat. Whisk gradually into egg yolks and sugar, return the mixture to the clean pan and heat gently, stirring constantly, until the mixture coats the back of a wooden spoon.

3 Stir in vanilla essence to taste. Fold in mango purée. Transfer mixture to a deep-sided metal container or polythene tub. Cover. Freeze until ice crystals form around the edge of the mixture, then beat with a hand-held electric mixer until smooth. Repeat this process twice more, then leave until solid. Alternatively, use an ice cream maker.

4 Transfer ice cream to the refrigerator 15 minutes before serving to allow it to soften slightly.

Serves 6-8

Left: *Marshmallow Surprises (page 71)*
Right: *Mango Ice Cream*

CHILLED LEMON ZABAGLIONE

6 egg yolks
¾ cup/185 g/6 oz caster sugar
1 tablespoon grated lemon rind
¼ cup/60 mL/2 fl oz lemon juice
2 tablespoons Marsala

1   Place egg yolks in a large heatproof bowl which fits over a saucepan. Add caster sugar, lemon rind, lemon juice and Marsala. Whisk with a hand-held electric mixer until mixture is light and fluffy.

2   Place the bowl over a saucepan of simmering water and continue to whisk for 8 minutes or until mixture thickens.

3   Remove bowl from pan. Continue to whisk the mixture for about 7 minutes more or until cool.

4   Pour zabaglione into four dessert glasses; chill until ready to serve.

Serves 4

ST CLEMENT'S SORBET

1¼ cups/300 mL/10 fl oz water
¾ cup/185 g/6 oz sugar
1 cup/250 mL/8 fl oz lemon juice
1 cup/250 mL/8 fl oz orange juice
grated rind of 1 orange
grated rind of 1 lemon
1 egg white

1   Combine water and sugar in a saucepan. Heat, stirring until all the sugar has dissolved, then bring to the boil. Boil for 5 minutes without stirring. Tip into a bowl, cool slightly, then stir in citrus juices and rinds.

2   Transfer mixture to a metal container or polythene tub. Cover. Freeze until ice crystals form around the edge of the mixture, then beat with a hand-held electric mixer until smooth.

3   Whisk egg white in a clean grease-free bowl until stiff but not dry; fold into semi-frozen mixture. Return the mixture to the freezer until solid, whisking once or twice more during freezing.

4   Transfer sorbet to the refrigerator about 15 minutes before serving, to allow it to soften slightly.

Serves 6

ICE CREAM ORANGES

6 large oranges
4 tablespoons orange liqueur
2 cups/500 mL/16 fl oz thickened cream (double)
¾ cup/125 g/4 oz icing sugar
1 tablespoon finely grated orange rind

1   Wash and dry oranges. Cut a sliver off the base of each, so that they stand level, then cut a deeper slice off the top of each orange. Reserve these slices as lids.

2   Squeeze oranges, taking care not to damage the shells. Remove as much of the compressed flesh and pith as possible to leave shells clean.

3   Arrange orange shells and lids on a baking sheet. Place carefully in the freezer.

4   Make filling. Tip ¾ cup/185 mL/ 6 fl oz of the orange juice into a measuring jug. Stir in liqueur. Place cream, icing sugar and orange rind in a bowl. Whip until cream starts to thicken. Trickle in orange juice mixture, beating constantly until cream forms soft peaks.

5   Spoon about half the flavoured cream into the chilled orange shells, piling it up in the centre. Return filled shells and lids to the freezer for 8-12 hours or until filling is firm. Chill the remaining flavoured cream in a covered bowl in the refrigerator.

6   Transfer filled shells to the refrigerator 15 minutes before serving, to allow the ice cream to soften slightly. Spoon the chilled cream into a piping bag fitted with a shell nozzle and pipe swirls of cream around the rim of six dessert plates. Arrange one of the filled oranges in the centre of each plate and top with an orange lid.

Serves 6

DOM PEDRO

4 cups/1 litre/1¾ pt good-quality vanilla ice cream
¼ cup/60 mL/2 fl oz thickened cream (double)
½ cup/125 mL/4 fl oz coffee liqueur

1   Scoop ice cream into a blender or food processor, in batches if

Minted Green Salad

necessary. Add the cream and liqueur and process briefly to mix. Pour into tall glasses and serve at once with straws and long-handled spoons.

Serves 4-6

MINTED GREEN SALAD

¼ cup/60 g/2 oz sugar
⅓ cup/90 mL/3 fl oz water
3 tablespoons mint liqueur
½ honeydew melon
185 g/6 oz seedless green grapes
1 Granny Smith apple
2 kiwifruit, peeled and chopped
mint sprigs and lime slices to
   decorate

1   Combine sugar and measured water in a saucepan. Heat, stirring until all the sugar has dissolved, then bring to the boil. Boil without stirring for 2-3 minutes. Tip into a bowl, cool slightly, then stir in liqueur.

2   Remove seeds from melon; using a melon baller scoop out flesh into a bowl. Add grapes. Cut apple into quarters, remove core from each piece and slice flesh into bowl. Add kiwifruit and mix lightly.

3   Pour syrup over and toss to combine. Cover and chill for at least 2 hours before serving, decorated with mint sprigs and lime slices.

Serves 4

MARSHMALLOW SURPRISES
Illustrated on page 68

20 firm round plain biscuits
10 squares chocolate
20 white marshmallows
20 pink marshmallows
20 small strawberries

1   Arrange half the biscuits on a baking sheet. Top each biscuit with a piece of chocolate. Thread pink and white marshmallows in pairs on long-handled forks or skewers.

2   When the fire has died down sufficiently to give off a gentle heat, toast marshmallows slowly until hot and gooey in the centre.

3   Using a spoon, push all the marshmallows onto chocolate-topped biscuits. Immediately complete each 'sandwich' by adding a plain biscuit. Press biscuits together carefully. The hot marshmallow will melt the chocolate to form a delicious filling. Transfer to a plate, add the straw-berries and serve, but take care when eating – the filling will be very hot at first.

Makes 10

MANDARIN AND KIWIFRUIT SALAD

¼ cup/60 mL/2 fl oz water
¼ cup/60 g/2 oz sugar
2 tablespoons finely chopped
   stem ginger
¼ cup/60 mL/2 fl oz orange juice
1 tablespoon lemon juice
1 tablespoon ginger wine
1 x 315 g/10 oz can mandarin
   oranges, drained
6 kiwifruit, peeled and sliced

1   Combine measured water and sugar in a saucepan. Heat, stirring until all the sugar has dissolved, then bring to the boil. Boil without stirring for 5 minutes. Tip into a bowl, cool slightly, then stir in ginger, orange juice, lemon juice and ginger wine. Leave to cool.

2   Tip mandarin oranges into a bowl. Add sliced kiwifruit and mix lightly. Pour over ginger mixture, cover and chill for at least 2 hours before serving.

Serves 6

PASSIONFRUIT TART

2½ cups/315 g/10 oz plain flour
1 tablespoon caster sugar
220 g/7 oz butter, cubed
¼ cup/60 mL/2 fl oz iced water
1 cup/250 mL/8 fl oz carton or
   canned custard
1 cup/250 mL/8 fl oz thickened
   cream (double)
4 tablespoons lemon juice
2 teaspoons powdered gelatine
4 tablespoons water
170 g/5½ oz fresh or canned
   passionfruit pulp
3 tablespoons icing sugar

1 Combine flour and caster sugar in a large bowl. Rub in butter with fingertips until mixture resembles fine breadcrumbs, then add iced water, drop by drop, until dough can be held together. Quickly knead into a ball, wrap and refrigerate for 30 minutes.

2 Preheat oven to 190°C, 375°F, Gas 5. Roll out dough on a lightly floured surface to fit a 23 cm/9 in flan dish. Line pastry case with nonstick baking paper. Fill with uncooked rice and cook for 10 minutes, then remove rice and paper and bake for 5 minutes more. Set pastry case aside to cool.

3 Mix custard, cream and half the lemon juice in a large bowl. Sprinkle gelatine over measured water in a cup. When spongy, melt over hot water. Stir into custard mixture, mixing well. Spoon mixture into pastry case. Refrigerate for 30 minutes.

4 Mix passionfruit pulp and remaining lemon juice in a saucepan. Stir in icing sugar. Cook for 5 minutes over moderate heat, stirring mixture constantly, then set aside to cool to room temperature.

5 Serve pie in wedges, topping each portion with a little of the cooled passionfruit sauce.

Serves 8

Cook's Tip: When adding the liquid gelatine to the custard mixture in either of these recipes, it is a good idea to begin by adding a little of the custard to the gelatine. This reduces the risk of the gelatine forming threads in the set pie filling.

ORANGE TARTLETS WITH CHOCOLATE ICE CREAM

½ x 220 g/7 oz packet frozen puff
   pastry, thawed
3 oranges
2 teaspoons powdered gelatine
¼ cup/60 mL/2 fl oz milk
1 cup/250 mL/8 fl oz carton or
   canned custard
1 tablespoon cointreau
½ cup/125 mL/4 fl oz thickened
   cream (double)
mint leaves to decorate
chocolate ice cream to serve

1 Preheat oven to 190°C, 375°F, Gas 5. Roll out pastry on a lightly floured surface and cut out four 7 cm/2¾ in rounds. Arrange on a lightly greased baking sheet and bake for 10 minutes or until risen and golden; set aside to cool.

2 Grate the rind of 1 orange into a small bowl. Squeeze the orange and set aside
2 tablespoons of the juice. Peel and segment the remaining oranges.

3 Sprinkle gelatine over milk in a cup. When spongy, melt over hot water. Place custard in a bowl and stir in gelatine, cointreau and reserved orange juice and grated orange rind.

4 In a separate bowl, whip cream until soft peaks form; fold into custard mixture. Cover and refrigerate for 25 minutes or until mixture begins to set.

5 Spread a little custard cream over each puff pastry round, leaving a 1 cm/½ in clear rim. Arrange orange segments on top. Decorate each tartlet with a mint leaf and serve on a dessert plate with a scoop of chocolate ice cream. Any remaining orange segments may be used as an additional decoration.

Serves 4

*Passionfruit Tart, Orange Tartlet with
Chocolate Ice Cream*

FRUIT KEBABS

6 bananas
¼ cup/60 mL/2 fl oz lemon juice
2 pears
12 drained canned apricot halves
12 drained canned pineapple
    chunks
6 strawberries, hulled
60 g/2 oz butter, melted
2 tablespoons soft light brown
    sugar

MARINADE
½ cup/125 mL/4 fl oz orange juice
2 tablespoons syrup from canned
    apricots or pineapple chunks
3 tablespoons brandy
1 tablespoon caster sugar
½ cinnamon stick
strip of orange rind

1 Make marinade by mixing orange juice, fruit syrup and 2 tablespoons of the brandy in a bowl. Stir in caster sugar and add cinnamon stick and orange rind.

2 Peel bananas and cut each one into six chunks. Place in a large bowl with lemon juice and toss gently. Halve and core, but do not peel, the pears. Cut into chunks, add to bananas and toss in lemon juice.

3 Add drained apricot halves, pineapple chunks and strawberries to the bowl. Pour over marinade and stir gently. Cover and marinate in the refrigerator for at least 2 hours.

4 Drain fruit, transferring marinade to a small saucepan. Thread banana and pear chunks, apricot halves, pineapple chunks and strawberries alternately onto 12 metal skewers. Alternatively, use wooden skewers which have been soaked in water.

5 Bring marinade to the boil, then transfer to the edge of the barbecue grill to keep warm. Brush fruit gently with melted butter and sprinkle with brown sugar. Cook on a lightly oiled barbecue grill over moderately hot coals for 6-8 minutes, turning frequently to ensure fruit does not char.

6 Add remaining brandy to marinade, pour into a heatproof jug and serve with the grilled fruit kebabs.

Serves 6

HAZELNUT ICE CREAM

90 g/3 oz hazelnuts
½ cup/125 g/4 oz caster sugar
1 cup/250 mL/8 fl oz thickened
    cream (double)
1 cup/250 mL/8 fl oz milk
½ teaspoon lemon juice

1 Preheat oven to 180°C, 350°F, Gas 4. Spread out hazelnuts in a roasting tin. Place in the oven until skins start to burst and nuts turn golden. Shake tin from time to time. Tip nuts onto a clean kitchen towel and rub off most of the skins.

2 Grind nuts in a food processor until very fine and oily, stopping once to scrape down sides. Add sugar, cream and milk and process until combined. With motor running, add lemon juice through feeder tube.

3 Transfer mixture to a deep-sided metal container or polythene tub. Cover. Freeze until ice crystals form around the edge of the mixture, then beat with a hand-held electric mixer until smooth. Repeat this process once more; then leave until solid. Alternatively, use an ice cream maker, and follow the manufacturer's instructions.

4 Transfer ice cream to the refrigerator 15 minutes before serving to allow it to soften slightly.

Serves 4

Fruit Kebabs

PECAN MERINGUE LAYERS WITH PEACHES

oil for greasing
60 g/2 oz pecan nuts or walnuts
6 peaches
6 egg whites
1¼ cups/315 g/10 oz caster sugar
2 cups/500 mL/16 fl oz thickened cream (double), whipped

1 Preheat oven to 180°C, 350°F, Gas 4. Trace three 23 cm/9 in circles on nonstick baking paper. Place circles on baking sheets and brush lightly with oil.

2 Spread out pecan nuts or walnuts in a roasting tin. Place in the oven until nuts are a deep golden brown. Shake tin from time to time and check the nuts frequently to ensure that they do not burn. Cool nuts slightly, then chop finely by hand or in a food processor. Lower oven temperature to 140°C, 275°F, Gas 1.

3 Place peaches in a heatproof bowl. Pour on boiling water to cover, leave for 2 minutes, then slip off peach skins. Drain, cut peaches in half and remove stones. Slice thinly.

4 Whip egg whites in a large grease-free bowl until soft peaks form. Add sugar, 1 tablespoon at a time, whipping after each addition until mixture is stiff and glossy. Fold in chopped nuts.

5 Spread meringue evenly over circles on baking paper. Bake for about 1¼ hours or until meringue layers are dry and crisp. Remove from oven and allow to cool on baking sheets for 10 minutes. Peel off baking paper and return meringues to turned off oven with door open to cool.

6 Spread two of the circles with cream and top with two thirds of the peach slices. Layer the circles together, place the third circle on top and decorate with swirls of cream and the remaining peach slices. Serve as soon as possible.

Serves 8

Flaming Bananas

FLAMING BANANAS

6 bananas
¾ cup/185 mL/6 fl oz orange juice
2 tablespoons grated orange rind
½ teaspoon grated nutmeg
90 g/3 oz butter
¼ cup/45 g/1½ oz soft light brown sugar
1 tablespoon orange liqueur
4 tablespoons rum
crème fraîche or Greek yogurt to serve

1 Peel bananas. Place in a shallow dish and spoon orange juice over the top. Sprinkle with orange rind and nutmeg. Set aside for 2-3 minutes.

2 Melt butter in a large frying pan set over a burner at the barbecue table, or place the pan on the barbecue grill over hot coals.

3 Stir in the sugar. Drain the orange juice mixture from the bananas and add it to the pan with the orange liqueur. Stir until the mixture is smooth and hot.

4 Add the bananas to the pan in a single layer. Cook until golden brown and tender, basting the bananas frequently with the sauce.

5 Heat the rum in a metal ladle over the barbecue or burner. Carefully ignite the rum and pour it over the bananas. Serve as soon as the flames have died down, offering crème fraîche or Greek yogurt as an accompaniment.

Serves 4

BARBECUE BASICS

The best barbecue cooks are made, not born. Man may have started out by rubbing two sticks together and roasting a rabbit, but there's more art than instinct in producing a perfectly cooked alfresco meal with the minimum of fuss. The more you know about this fascinating method of cooking, the less likely you are to produce a burnt offering.

◆ ◆ ◆

THE BARBECUE

While it is perfectly possible to cook on a simple arrangement of bricks topped with a rack from Granny's old oven, it is a lot easier, and more convenient, to buy a freestanding barbecue that fits your family's needs, or to turn part of your garden into an area for outdoor entertaining by building in a barbecue.

The range of barbecues available can be bewildering, from simple disposables to sophisticated cooking centres complete with warming ovens, often fuelled by gas or electricity. If you are new to this type of cooking, the best advice is to start small. Invest in a relatively inexpensive compact grill or hibachi (a simple table-top or freestanding cast-iron or aluminium barbecue) or buy an inexpensive brazier. Usually rectangular, but sometimes round, a brazier is basically a firebox on legs. It has vents or dampers in the base to control the flow of air to the burning coals, and an adjustable grill, so that you can control the cooking temperature by altering the distance of the food from the fire. Some braziers have windbreaks or hinged lids, and more sophisticated models include a rotisserie. It is usual for two of the legs on the brazier to be fitted with wheels. The remaining legs provide an anchor when the barbecue is stationary, but it can easily be moved. This enables you to experiment to find the best place in your garden for cooking, a discovery which will prove invaluable if you later decide to build in a permanent barbecue.

Kettles are circular bowls with domed hoods that reflect the heat and promote faster cooking. They are versatile appliances, as suitable for cooking a few sausages as they are for the longer, slower cooking required for a chicken or joint. The cooking temperature is regulated by dampers which control the air flow to the burning coals.

Campers and hikers will find disposable barbecues a boon. These consist of aluminium trays filled with ready-to-light charcoal and fitted with a mesh grid. Take care to use them only in places where it is safe (and permitted) to do so, and dispose of them in the approved manner.

A built-in barbecue can become a real feature of the garden, but must be properly planned. The ideal site is one that is close enough to the kitchen for convenience but away from any overhanging trees or shrubs. Choose a sheltered position and bear in mind the prevailing wind: any smoke generated should be carried away from the seating area – but not onto your neighbour's patio! Experimenting with a portable barbecue will enable you to find the perfect spot.

You don't have to be a bricklayer to build a barbecue – kits make the process reasonably painless, and you may enjoy the exercise so much that you will find yourself adding a food preparation area, a bar counter and even built-in seating. The important thing to remember is to allow plenty of room around the actual fireplace for the cook to work in safety, and to enable guests to feel part of the proceedings. The grill should be at a comfortable height, and you should be able to adjust its distance from the coals. Good lighting is important – you don't want to be limited to barbecuing during the day, and flashing a torch on

a piece of meat is no way to test whether it is cooked sufficiently.

FUEL

Barbecues fuelled by bottled gas are efficient and speedy. Lava rocks heated by gas burners produce an even heat, and if you have multiple burners you may even be able to vary the temperature on different areas of the grill. This is particularly helpful if you wish to cook steaks at the same time as chicken breasts, for instance, which require a more gentle heat.

Electric barbecues also produce instant and easily controlled heat. They are ideal for people who wish to cook indoors and are sometimes incorporated into the design of sophisticated kitchens.

Charcoal-fuelled barbecues, however, remain the most popular type. Briquettes are slightly more expensive than lump charcoal, but they burn for longer and at a more consistent temperature.

Many barbecue buffs swear by cooking over a log fire, but not all of us are fortunate enough to have access to dry, well-seasoned wood. If this is the case, you can cheat a little and create a woody flavour by adding hickory or apple chips to hot charcoal. Dried rosemary branches work in much the same way and give off a wonderful aroma. Hardwoods,

such as oak, beech or ash, burn down to hot, evenly glowing coals, but softwoods should be saved for kindling - they burn too quickly to be of value as coals. Avoid using resinous woods like pine, as they give the food a strong taste reminiscent of turpentine.

LIGHTING-UP TIME

Purists take pride in laying a wood fire, constructing a tepee of twigs and other kindling, such as pine cones or twists of paper, setting this alight, and then adding progressively larger pieces of wood. The aim of the tepee is to allow air to circulate around the burning material, and a similar pyramid method works well for charcoal, when the process may be facilitated by the addition of a few solid firelighters between the coals. Take care when using solid or liquid fire starters. Always follow the directions to the letter and never use any other inflammable liquids. Appalling accidents have resulted when dangerous fluids have been poured onto fires. If you are a beginner in the barbecue stakes, or feel nervous about laying and lighting a fire, try using self-starting briquettes. These come sealed in a paper sack which is laid in the firebox of your barbecue. All you do is to set a match to the paper.

One of the most efficient kettle barbecues on the market has a perforated wide metal tube into which the briquettes are placed before ignition. Kindling in the form of twisted newspaper is placed in a removable bowl at the base of the barbecue, a couple of firelighters are added, and the filled metal tube is placed vertically on a grid immediately above the kindling, which is then lit. The kindling ignites the briquettes, which burn swiftly and evenly; within 30-40 minutes they will be ready for spreading, which is easy to achieve by means of handles on either side of the fuel tube. When the barbecue is over, it is a simple matter to sweep the cold ashes into the removable bowl for disposal.

The shape of the fire depends on what you intend to cook. A closely packed (but not solid) bed of coals gives an even, intense heat which is best for cooking sausages or small cuts of meat or poultry, while coals should be spread if a more gentle heat is required, as when cooking fish. When using a rotisserie, or cooking a joint of meat, it is usual to arrange the coals in a ring with the area immediately under the food occupied by a drip pan.

Before using a gas barbecue check that all the gas fittings and hose connections are tight. Follow the manufacturer's instructions for lighting. If the barbecue does not ignite immediately, turn it off, wait 20 seconds to allow any gas to disperse, then try again.

ACCESSORIES

Acquiring a barbecue doesn't mean that you have to spend a fortune on accessories, but there are some implements and items of equipment which no alfresco cook should lack:

- boards and sharp knives for the preparation of food and for carving meat after cooking. Always wash boards and knives thoroughly after each use; never cut up cooked meat on a board which has been used for raw (and vice versa)

- sturdy flameproof apron for spills and as a protection from sparks or spitting fat

- oven mitts for handling hot skewers, racks and frying pans

- hinged grills for holding burgers, fish steaks – even sandwiches – securely, enabling them to be turned over with one flip of the wrist. Oil grills lightly before use

- hinged baskets for whole fish: shaped ones are best as they do not compress the fish too much

- basting brush – a new paintbrush with firmly attached bristles (not plastic) works well

- long-handled tongs – one for moving the coals and another for turning food

- long-handled spatulas for turning delicate foods

- skewers – wooden or bamboo ones are good for lightweight ingredients like fish and mushrooms, but must be soaked in water before use. Metal skewers are better for meats

- water pistol or plant spray filled with water – use sparingly for dousing flare-ups and quenching the coals when cooking is complete. Any coals that have not burnt out can be allowed to dry and then used for the next barbecue

- foil (preferably heavy-duty) has a multitude of uses, from protecting the thin ends of meat from burning while thicker parts continue to cook, to making a drip tray to place beneath a joint of meat. A carefully sealed foil package is perfect for delicate cuts of fish, poultry, sliced vegetables and fruits.

GOOD COOKING

You have only to glance through this book to appreciate the wide variety of foods that can be cooked successfully on a barbecue. Alongside the obvious – sausages, hamburgers and chicken drumsticks – you will find suggestions for grilling fish and seafood, paupiettes, poultry skewers and satays, steaks, chops and whole joints of meat, plus vegetables, breads and even desserts. Marinades and sauces are widely used and there are plenty of tips for successful cooking.

The type and density of the food governs the temperature at which it should be cooked, and the duration of the cooking time. Intense heat is required for steaks, while fish, tender cuts of poultry and most vegetables benefit from being cooked over a gentler heat. Raise the grill to lower the cooking temperature, or spread out the coals.

Novice barbecue cooks often make the mistake of starting to cook too soon, when the fire is still so fierce that flare-ups become unavoidable. When the coals are ready they will be ash-grey all over, with glowing red hearts which will be clearly visible at night.

As a rough guide to the temperature of the coals, place your hand carefully above them, at a distance of about 15 cm/6 in. If you have to snatch your hand away after 3 seconds, the coals can be termed hot; if you can maintain the position for 5-7 seconds the coals are moderate, while low coals should allow you to hold the position for about 10 seconds. The cooling fire is ideal for the cooking of fruit kebabs or other desserts.

Keep flare-ups to a minimum by trimming excess fat from meat. Apply oil-based bastes carefully, preferably towards the end of the cooking time, and try to avoid dripping on the hot coals. If you need to maintain a fire over a long period (as when cooking a joint) it may be helpful to start a second 'feeder' barbecue a short while after lighting the first. This is preferable to adding cold coals to a hot fire, which would lower the temperature considerably.

HYGIENE AND SAFETY

When preparing food for the barbecue, avoid handling raw and cooked meat at the same time or with the same utensils, as this might lead to the transfer of bacteria. Any utensils or boards used should be washed thoroughly in hot soapy water before being dried and reused or put away. Wash your hands before preparing food and again after touching raw meat. Store meat, fish and poultry in the refrigerator, taking great care that blood does not drip onto other foods. Keep raw foods chilled until just before cooking, when they should be brought to room temperature. Serve barbecued food as soon as it is cooked.

Take care when cooking on the barbecue. Choose a safe site with good lighting and ventilation. If you use a fire starter, make sure that it is a safe proprietary product and follow the instructions on the packaging. Make sure that a responsible adult is in charge of the barbecue, and never leave the fire unattended. Pets and small children should be kept away from the immediate vicinity. Protect hands with oven mitts and clothing with an apron, and use long-handled barbecue tools for turning meat and moving coals.

Smother or douse the fire after cooking. Clean the barbecue after every use. Before putting it away for the winter, apply a light coating of oil to parts which might otherwise rust.

INDEX

ACKNOWLEDGMENTS
The publishers would like to thank the following for supplying props for photography in Australia:
Villa Italiana; Les Olivades; Mondo Cane; Fred Pazotti; Modern Living; The Parterre Garden; Balmain Garden Centre; Butler & Co; The Bay Tree; Corso de Fiori

STYLING
Carolyn Feinberg

Includes Index
ISBN 1 86343 206 X

Published by J.B. Fairfax Press Pty Ltd
80-82 McLachlan Avenue
Rushcutters Bay 2100
NSW Australia

Print and Colour separation by Cronion SA, Spain

Distributed by
J.B. Fairfax Press Pty Ltd
9 Trinity Centre, Park Farm Estate
Wellingborough, Northants NN8 6ZB
Tel: (01933) 402330
Fax: (01933) 402234